FOUNDATIONS OF INTERNAL ALCHEMY

Wang Mu

# Foundations
# of Internal Alchemy

## The Taoist Practice of Neidan

Translated and edited by

Fabrizio Pregadio

Golden Elixir Press

Originally published as "*Wuzhen pian* danfa yaozhi" 「悟真篇」丹法要旨

© 2011 Golden Elixir Press
ISBN 978-0984308255 (pbk)

Golden Elixir Press, Mountain View, CA
www.goldenelixir.com

# Contents

# Foreword

This book was originally published in 1982 as a two-part essay in *Zhongguo daojiao* (Chinese Taoism), the official journal of the China Taoist Association. In slightly revised forms, it was republished in 1990 as a lengthy appendix to an annotated edition of the *Wuzhen pian* (Awakening to Reality), entitled *Wuzhen pian qianjie* (A simple explanation of the *Wuzhen pian*); and again in 1990 in the author's collected writings, entitled *Neidan yangsheng gongfa zhiyao* (Foundations of the practices of Internal Alchemy and Nourishing Life), with several later reprints.

The author, Wang Mu 王沐 (1908–92), received the Longmen ordination in his youth. He taught Internal Alchemy (Neidan) and was held in high regard by both practitioners and Taoist scholars. He served as a board member of the China Taoist Association and was for some time in charge of its research activities. He is known outside China mainly for the above-mentioned edition of the *Wuzhen pian*, the text at the basis of the outline of Internal Alchemy that he provides in the present book.

As all readers will notice, Wang Mu writes from the viewpoint of his tradition. He accepts virtually all traditional details concerning such issues as doctrine, lineage, and textual authorship or date. In many cases, he essentially rephrases statements found in the original texts into present-day language. His procedure is also analogous to the one seen in the textual sources of Neidan, which repeatedly quote passages of earlier writings taking them as positive and definitive evidence of the validity of their own assertions. The recurrent articulation of certain basic concepts is another feature shared with the original Neidan texts.

Except for the introduction and the short conclusion, Wang Mu's work is arranged according to the stages of the alchemical practice: a preliminary phase followed by three main stages. For each stage, the focus of Wang Mu's discourse, which makes his work extremely valuable, is the discussion of the main relevant terms and concepts, including such essential notions as Essence, Breath, and Spirit; the "fire times" (*huohou*); and the Embryo. With regard to this point, an additional trait that his discussion shares with the alchemical texts is the progressively shorter space devoted to each stage. As Li Daochun (ca. 1290) wrote in one of his works, when the alchemical practice comes to the third and last stage, "no words apply."

As a writer, Wang Mu makes very few concessions to his reader, and none specifically to his Western reader: his work is written for, and addressed to, a Chinese audience. Although he provides an accessible overview of Internal Alchemy, mainly focused on its practices, he does not intend in the first place to popularize, but to transmit. This feature has been preserved in the present English translation: with the exception of a few footnotes that attempt to clarify certain points probably taken for granted by a Chinese reader, but possibly equivocal for a Western reader, the translation tries to reproduce as closely as possible the author's own writing style and line of reasoning. References to sources, which Wang Mu as a rule does not provide, have been supplied for all quotations that have been identified.

One final point that requires consideration in reading Wang Mu's work is directly related to its date of publication. In the People's Republic of China, during the 1980s, Taoism had just begun to recover from the trials endured in the previous decades, making good use of a limited easing of controls by the central government. Several works published in those years present Neidan as a form of Qigong, in an effort to circumvent restraints on what was still official labeled as a "feudal superstition." This may explain Wang Mu's frequent stress on the merits of Neidan in relation to medicine and healing, his repeated references to the "scientific" evidence of its benefits, and the value he accords to the practitioner's "active" attitude, suggesting that the Neidan practice does not necessarily imply a lack of involvement in society. Certain terms and notions occasionally used in the book—e.g., "materialism" and "subjective idealism"—are best seen as the price to pay in order to be entitled to write on more significant subjects.

Fabrizio Pregadio
February 2011

Part 1

# INTRODUCTION

# The Basis:

# Essence and Spirit

The work entitled *Awakening to Reality* (*Wuzhen pian*), written by Zhang Boduan around 1075, has been included in the Taoist Canon, in the Buddhist Canon, and in several collections compiled by Confucian scholars under imperial decree.[1] The *Siku tiyao* (Descriptive Notes on the Books of the Four Repositories) states that, with Wei Boyang's *Cantong qi* (Token for the Joining of the Three), *Awakening to Reality* contains the orthodox transmission of the Taoist alchemical methods. In the table of contents of his *Daozang jinghua lu* (Record of the Essential Splendors of the Taoist Canon), Ding Fubao (1874–1952) praises *Awakening to Reality* saying: "Its words are smooth and fluent, and its meaning is deep and profound. This work contains the golden rule to cultivate the Elixir, the jade principle to give nourishment to life."

This shows that *Awakening to Reality* has been held in high esteem within all the Three Teachings: Taoism, Confucianism, and Buddhism. With regard to Neidan (Internal Alchemy), Zhang Boduan's work inherits and transmits the principles of self-cultivation of the *Cantong qi*, and provides a synopsis of the doctrines of the period prior to the Song dynasty (960–1279). However, *Awakening to Reality* is addressed to those who have already attained a rather deep level of attainment in the practices of Neidan (Internal Alchemy). Therefore Zhang Boduan's work does not begin from the basic methods, and does not provide a systematic arrangement of the stages of the alchemical practice. In addition, its poems are obscure and do not follow a precise sequence. This is done intentionally, so that those who read the text for the first time may perceive its profundity.

---

[1] The Buddhist Canon of the Qing period (*Qianlong Dazang jing*) contains the Yongzheng Emperor's *Yuxuan yulu* (Imperial Compilation of Recorded Sayings), which in turn includes a partial version of the "Outer Chapters" of the *Wuzhen pian*. See also below, p. 111.

While *Awakening to Reality* does not deal with the initial stage of the practice, details on this subject are found in three other works by Zhang Boduan. One of them, the *Secret Text of Green Florescence* (*Qinghua biwen*), contains a systematic exposition of oral instructions on the foundations of the practice. The other two, namely the *Four Hundred Words on the Golden Elixir* (*Jindan sibai zi*) and the *Book of the Eight Vessels* (*Bamai jing*), give concrete details on the initial stage.[2]

These works supply what is missing in *Awakening to Reality*. The present book will look at the four texts together and present their content in a systematic way. This will make it possible to proceed without ambiguities from the surface to the core, and present an outline of Zhang Boduan's alchemical practice. The broader integration of these notions lies in the hands of the reader: the present book can do no more than providing some clues, and should be used only as a source of information.

*Nature (Xing) and Life (Ming).* With regard to the alchemical practice, *Awakening to Reality* maintains that the cultivation of Ming (Life) should precede the cultivation of Xing (Nature), and that "doing" (*youwei*) should precede "non-doing" (*wuwei*). Of course, this does not mean that, at the beginning of the practice, one receives only instructions on compounding the Elixir, and that nothing at all is conveyed on the cultivation of the mind: each stage of the practice gives emphasis to one or the other aspect, but neither should be cultivated on its own.

Zhang Boduan's works show that, in his view, the first stage of the alchemical practice ("laying the foundations") consists of the dual cultivation of Xing (Nature) and Ming (Life). The second stage ("refining Essence to transmute it into Breath") emphasizes the work on Ming. In the third stage ("refining Breath to transmute it into Spirit"), the work on Xing has priority on the work on Ming. Finally, in the fourth stage ("refining Spirit to return to Emptiness") one works only on Xing. Whether the cultivation of Xing or of Ming has priority depends, in other words, on the progress of one's practice. However, while the first stage is described in Zhang Boduan's three other works, *Awakening to Reality* begins from the second stage. In this work, therefore, the practice of Ming comes first, and the practice of Xing comes second. Then, in the "Outer

---

[2] *Author's note*: The *Secret Text of Green Florescence* was written by Zhang Boduan and edited by his disciple, Wang Bangshu. — The complete title of this work is *Yuqing jinsi Qinghua biwen jinbao neilian danjue* (Alchemical Instructions on the Inner Refinement of the Golden Treasure, a Secret Text from the Golden Casket of the Jade Clarity Transmitted by the Immortal of Green Florescence).

Chapters" ("Waipian") of *Awakening to Reality*, Zhang Boduan presents a series of poems based on the principles of Chan (Zen) Buddhism. He uses those principles as metaphors for the practice of Xing, in order to assist the students in their comprehension of the ultimate foundation.

*Imagery and language.* Before we begin, a few remarks are necessary on the approach required to read *Awakening to Reality*. This text cannot be studied on the basis of the superficial meanings of its words. In his *Sizhu Wuzhen pian* (Four Commentaries to *Awakening to Reality*), Fu Jinquan (1765–1844) says:

> 丹經有微言，有顯言，有正言，有疑似之言，有比喻之言，有影射之言，有旁敲側擊之言，有丹理，有口訣，似神龍隱現，出沒不測，東露一鱗，西露一爪，所以讀者必須細心尋求也。

> In the alchemical texts there are subtle words, plain words, clear words, allusive words, metaphoric words, murky words, as well as circuitous and cunning words. There are doctrines on the Elixir, and there are oral instructions. It is as if a divine dragon first hides itself and then emerges, only to vanish and become invisible again, leaving a scale on the eastern road, and a claw on the western road. This requires much attention from the reader.

*Awakening to Reality* itself says:

> 卦中設象本儀形，得象忘言意自明，舉世迷徒惟執象，卻行卦氣望飛昇。

> The images of the hexagrams are established on the basis of their
>     meanings:
> understand the images and forget the words — the idea is clear of
>     itself.
> The whole world delusively clings to the images:
> they practice the "breaths of the hexagrams" and hope thereby to
>     rise in flight.[3]

This tells the readers that they should not try to to understand the core by looking at the surface, or they would be caught in a maze. They should, instead, look at the front, the back, the cracks, and the edges to

---

[3]  *Wuzhen pian*, "Jueju," poem 37. For comments on this poem, see p. 85.

find the true meaning; and they should draw the main gist from the "metaphoric, murky, and allusive words."

Weng Baoguang (fl. 1173) lists several dozen synonyms of Essence and Spirit.[4] The synonyms of Essence (*jing*) include the following:

| | |
|---|---|
| Kan ☵ | 坎 |
| *Geng* | 庚 |
| 4 | 四 |
| 9 | 九 |
| Metal | 金 |
| *Po*-Soul of the Moon | 月魄 |
| Hare's Lard | 兔脂 |
| Old Gentleman | 老郎 |
| Male Kan ☵ | 坎男 |
| True Lead | 真铅 |
| White Snow | 白雪 |
| Golden Liquor | 金液 |
| Water Tiger | 水虎 |
| Golden Flower | 金華 |
| Black Lead | 黑鉛 |
| Mother of the Elixir | 丹母 |
| Jade Pistil | 玉蕊 |
| Breath of the Tiger's Moon-Quarter | 虎弦氣 |
| Lead of the Yellow Sprout | 黃芽鉛 |
| Essence of the Black Turtle | 黑龜精 |
| Red Sun in the Pool's Bottom | 潭底日紅 |
| Gentleman in Plain Silk | 素練郎君 |
| White-haired Old Man | 白頭老子 |
| White within the Black | 黑中有白 |
| Half Pound of Hare's Marrow | 兔髓半斤 |
| Born at *Ren* and *Gui* | 生于壬癸 |
| Gentleman of 9 and 3 | 九三郎君 |
| Half-pound of Metal in the First Moon-Quarter | 上弦金半斤 |
| Moon-Essence of Wu in Kan ☵ | 坎戊月精 |

The synonyms of Spirit (*shen*) include the following:

| | |
|---|---|
| Li ☲ | 離 |

---

4   *Wuzhen zhizhi xiangshuo sansheng biyao*, "Jindan faxiang."

| | |
|---|---|
| *Mao* | 卯 |
| *Jia* | 甲 |
| East | 東 |
| 3 | 三 |
| 8 | 八 |
| Wood | 木 |
| *Hun*-Soul of the Sun | 日魂 |
| Marrow of the Crow | 烏髓 |
| Lovely Maiden | 姹女 |
| Green Beauty | 青娥 |
| True Mercury | 真汞 |
| Liquor of Wood | 木液 |
| Mercury of Fire | 火汞 |
| Fire Dragon | 火龍 |
| Metal Crow | 金烏 |
| Female Mother | 雌母 |
| Flowing Pearls | 流珠 |
| Red Lead | 紅鉛 |
| Vermilion Sand | 朱砂 |
| Joined Peaches | 交梨 |
| Jade Mushroom | 玉芝 |
| True Fire | 真火 |
| Silver in Water | 水銀 |
| Crow in the Sun | 日中烏 |
| Breath of the Dragon's Moon-Quarter | 龍弦氣 |
| Marrow of the Red Phoenix | 赤鳳髓 |
| Mercury in the Sand | 砂裏汞 |
| *Ji* within Li ☲ | 離之己 |
| White Moon on the Mountain's Peak | 山頭月白 |
| Woman in Green Attire | 青衣女子 |
| Barbarian with Jade-Blue Eyes | 碧眼胡兒 |
| Eight Ounces of Crow's Liver | 烏肝八兩 |
| Born at *Bing* and *Ding* | 生于丙丁 |
| Lovely Maiden of the Two Eights | 二八姹女 |
| Vermilion Sand in the Tripod | 朱砂鼎內 |
| Half-pound of Water in the Last Moon-Quarter | 下弦水半斤 |

In fact, those listed above are only a small part of the code names of Essence and Spirit; but they clearly illustrate the fact that the large variety of terms used in the alchemical texts serves to intentionally conceal the true teachings. Now, if the main purpose of a religious teaching is drawing people to faith, why are the alchemical texts so obscure? Essentially, the Taoist alchemical methods are kept secret within closed groups; the selection of disciples is severe, and the methods are transmitted under oath. The most important points are not committed to writing: they are handed down in person from master to disciple, and are transmitted by word of mouth. Therefore when the alchemical masters write their books, they are extremely cautious. As the saying goes, they hide the mother and talk of the son, and leave the root to pursue the branches. Their writings are more complex than riddles.

Nevertheless, if a reader effectively understands the points of crucial importance, and discerns the clues that reveal the overall pattern, the alchemical texts are not too hard to comprehend. This is because the metaphors used in the texts consist only of the images of the eight trigrams (*bagua*), the sequences of "generation and conquest" (*shengke*) of the five agents, the numbers of the *Chart of the Yellow River* (*Hetu*), and the terminology of Waidan (External Alchemy); they include terms related to the alchemical laboratory and to the vegetal world, borrow from the transformations of Yin and Yang displayed by the Sun and Moon, and refer to the features of the cycle of the four seasons during the year.

Below the surface, when the alchemical texts provide the true instructions, they simply take Essence, Breath, and Spirit as the foundation. By means of the practice, Essence, Breath, and Spirit are transmuted; they gather in the Cinnabar Field, and coagulate and coalesce together. Afterward, by "sitting in quiescence" and "harmonizing the breathing," and by using the Intention (*yi*) as a guide, one's practice progressively deepens, and this allows the internal organs and the bones to be filled with energy. Breath and blood flow unobstructed, the natural potential of one's own life force develops, and this can heal from illnesses and defer decline and aging. Therefore, although the alchemical texts use a large number of metaphors to provide their discourse with a spiritual quality, the discourse itself is not otherworldly. It consists, rather, in a method for Nourishing Life (*yangsheng*) based on a hard practice of inner refining.

Taoist thought is idealistic, but its spirit is positive: it resides in an attempt to regulate the cosmos and control nature. The saying, "inverting the course generates an Immortal" (*nixing chengxian*) does not only apply to one's own practice, but to the whole view of the cosmos: "inverting the course" means reversing the ordinary patterns, so that all things return under the command of the alchemical master.

The Taoist ideal is calling the wind and summoning the rain, transforming the four seasons, giving commands to the spirits, and returning to life after death. With regard to the human body, Taoism considers that we can use our natural functions to heal from illness, and a self-cultivation practice to defer aging and reach a long life. In the words of the *Yinfu jing* (Scripture of the Hidden Agreement):

宇宙在乎手，萬化生乎身。

The cosmos lies in your hands, the ten thousand transformations are born from yourself.[5]

*Awakening to Reality* is filled with this religious spirit. While this may be called a fantasy, it is because of that spirit that, in the view of Zhang Boduan's work, one can attain a long life, provided that the alchemical practice is performed in the appropriate way. A poem in *Awakening to Reality* says:

藥逢氣類方成象，道在希夷合自然，一粒靈丹吞入腹，始知我命不由天。

Only when the Medicines meet in breath (*qi*) and kind do they form an image:
the Dao is inaudible and invisible, and is joined to What is so by Itself.
Ingest the one grain of numinous Elixir, let it enter the belly,
and for the first time you will know that your destiny does not depend on Heaven.[6]

This poem reflects the positive spirit of the entire text. We cannot deny that this attitude amounts to a form of subjective idealism; but in spite of that, the poem shows that, while the final goal of Taoism is "non-doing" (*wuwei*), the process of self-cultivation involves actual and substantial "doing" (*youwei*). In the alchemical methods of the Southern Lineage (Nanzong), this corresponds to the view that the practice should first use a "gradual method" (*jianfa*), which follows a definite sequence of steps and stages; and then use an "immediate method" (*dunfa*), by which, after a certain stage, it produces instantaneous results. Concerning this point, *Awakening to Reality* says:

---

[5]  *Yinfu jing*, part 1.
[6]  *Wuzhen pian*, "Jueju," poem 54.

始於有作人難見，及至無為眾始知，但見無為為要妙，豈知有作
是根基。

It begins with *doing*, and hardly can one see a thing,
when it comes to *non-doing*, all begin to understand.
But if you only see *non-doing* as the essential marvel,
how can you know that *doing* is the foundation?[7]

The entire alchemical practice is inspired by and revolves around this
way of seeing. The practices of *Awakening to Reality* consist in restoring,
replenishing, augmenting, and furthering the bodily functions in order to
reach a higher state of health.

Among the alchemical texts attributed to Zhang Boduan, *Awakening
to Reality* is certainly his own work. Two other texts, namely the *Secret
Text of Green Florescence* and the *Four Hundred Words on the Golden Elixir*, are
included in the Taoist Canon, while the *Book of the Eight Vessels* was incorporated by Li Shizhen (1518–93) in his *Bencao gangmu* (Pharmacopoeia
Arranged into Headings and Subheadings). The origins of the latter three
texts are clear, and their transmission is identical: all of them belong to
the Pure Cultivation branch (Qingxiu pai) of the Southern Lineage of
Neidan. Yu Yan (1258–1314) was the first to suspect that the *Four Hundred
Words* was composed by Bai Yuchan (1194–1229?), and some believe that
the *Secret Text of Green Florescence* was actually written by Li Buye during
the Ming period. These assumptions, however, are devoid of sufficient
testimony and are not supported by adequate evidence.

On the whole, the Taoist alchemical practices constitute one type of
methods of Nourishing Life (*yangsheng*). If one not only studies, but also
performs those practices, removing the religious coloring and the fantasies of "long life," then the specific methods of operation are worthy of
attention.

---

[7] *Wuzhen pian*, "Jueju," poem 42.

Part 2

# STAGES OF
# THE ALCHEMICAL PRACTICE
# IN *AWAKENING TO REALITY*

# The Four Stages

In the Zhong-Lü tradition, the description of the alchemical practice is generally divided into four stages: (1) Laying the foundations; (2) Refining Essence to transmute it into Breath; (3) Refining Breath to transmute it into Spirit; (4) Refining Spirit to return to Emptiness.

The main features of the four stages are the following:

1   "Laying the foundations" (*zhuji*) is the practice performed to replenish the Three Origins (*sanyuan*, i.e., Original Essence, Original Breath, and Original Spirit) within the body.

2   "Refining Essence to transmute it into Breath" (*lianjing huaqi*) is the "initial barrier" (*chuguan*) of inner cultivation. At this stage, Original Essence, Original Breath, and Original Spirit coagulate with one another and form a Breath made of the union of Essence and Breath. This stage is also called Compounding the Great Medicine (*zuo dayao*).

3   "Refining Breath to transmute it into Spirit" (*lianqi huashen*) is the "intermediate barrier" (*zhongguan*) of inner cultivation. The Great Medicine coagulates with Original Spirit, and they form a Spirit made of the union of the Three Origins. This stage is also called Compounding the Elixir (*zuodan*).

4   "Refining Spirit to return to Emptiness" (*lianshen huanxu*) is the "higher barrier" (*shangguan*) of inner cultivation. By refining Spirit one attains Emptiness and Non-Being (*xuwu*). This is the highest state.

The following chapters describe the four stages in detail.

# 1    "Laying the Foundations"

The expression "laying the foundations" is a metaphor often used in the alchemical texts. To build a house, one must first lay the foundations. Only when the foundations are stable and firm is it possible to set pillars and beams in place, and arrange bricks and tiles. Refining the Internal Elixir is based on the same principle.

The alchemical practice, however, is concerned with the human body. At the initial stage of the Neidan process, therefore, one should first replenish the basic constituents of the body, so that they conform to the requirements of the practice. Only then is it possible to undertake the stages of alchemical refinement proper. Until the basic constituents do not conform to those requirements, the body's functions should be restored and augmented by means of inner practices, so that Essence, Breath, and Spirit can reach a state of abundance. All this pertains to the stage of "laying the foundations."

Taoism deems Essence, Breath, and Spirit to be the major components of life, and the alchemical texts call them the Three Treasures (*sanbao*). If the Three Treasures are healthy and flourishing, the body is strong; if they are drained and depleted, illnesses develop. When the alchemical texts speak of refining the Elixir, they actually mean refining the Three Treasures. Chen Zhixu (1290–ca. 1368) says in his *Jindan dayao* (Great Essentials of the Golden Elixir):

> 神氣精三物相感，順則成人，逆則生丹。何謂順？一生二，二生三，三生萬物，故虛化神，神化氣，氣化精，精化形，形乃成人。何謂逆？萬物含三，三歸二，二歸一。知此道者，怡神守形，養形鍊精，積精化氣，鍊氣合神，鍊神還虛，金丹乃成。

Essence, Breath, and Spirit affect one another. When they follow the course, they form the human being; when they invert the course, they generate the Elixir.

What is the meaning of "following the course" (*shun*)? "The One generates the Two, the Two generate the Three, the Three generate

15

the ten thousand things."[1] Therefore Emptiness transmutes itself into Spirit, Spirit transmutes itself into Breath, Breath transmutes itself into Essence, Essence transmutes itself into form, and form becomes the human being.

What is the meaning of "inverting the course" (ni)? The ten thousand things hold the Three, the Three return to the Two, the Two return to the One. Those who know this Way look after their Spirit and guard their corporeal form. They nourish the corporeal form to refine the Essence, accumulate the Essence to transmute it into Breath, refine the Breath to merge it with Spirit, and refine the Spirit to revert to Emptiness. Then the Golden Elixir is achieved.[2]

In his commentary to *Awakening to Reality*, Weng Baoguang writes:

精能生氣，氣能生神，榮衛一身，莫大於此。養生之士，先寶其精，精滿則氣壯，氣壯則神旺，神旺則身健而少病。內則五藏敷華，外則皮膚潤澤。顏容光彩，耳目聰明。

Essence can generate Breath, and Breath can generate Spirit; to strengthen and protect oneself, nothing is more important than this. Those who devote themselves to Nourishing Life (*yangsheng*) treasure in the first place their Essence. If the Essence is full, Breath is strong; if the Breath is strong, Spirit flourishes; if the Spirit flourishes, the body is healthy and there are few illnesses. Internally, the five viscera bloom; externally, the skin becomes smooth. One's complexion is luminous, and one's ears and eyes are sharp and bright.[3]

In the two passages quoted above, Chen Zhixu explains Essence, Breath, and Spirit in terms of their sequence in "following the course" and "inverting the course." Weng Baoguang, instead, explains them as the basic components of existence. But beyond these differences, at the stage of "laying the foundations" there are two tasks: the first is preserving the state of Essence and Breath; the second is replenishing their shortage. When Essence is abundant, when Breath is full, and when Spirit is flourishing, this stage of the practice is concluded.

---

[1] *Daode jing*, 42.
[2] *Jindan dayao*, chapter 4.
[3] Only the first sentence of this passage is found in Weng Baoguang's *Wuzhen pian zhushu*, chapter 1. The remainder is actually a quotation from Chen Zhixu's *Jindan dayao*, chapter 3. Both passages are attributed to Weng Baoguang in the Qing-dynasty *Yangsheng sanyao* (The Three Essentials for Nourishing Life).

*"Superior virtue" and "inferior virtue."* At the stage of "laying the founda-tions," there are differences of initial conditions, age, and physical constitution. The practices, therefore, differ according to each individual. With regard to this point, the alchemical texts distinguish between "superior virtue" (*shangde*) and "inferior virtue" (*xiade*). "Superior virtue" refers to childhood and young age; "inferior virtue" refers to adulthood and old age.

According to the principles of alchemy, at a young age the human body grows like a young sprout. Borrowing a term from the *Daode jing* (Book of the Way and its Virtue), this is called "superior virtue."[4] Spirit and Breath are abundant, and there is no need of performing any practice to build the foundations. After growth and maturity, Essence, Breath, and Spirit become consumed and should be replenished. In the alchemical practice, this is referred to as "inferior virtue": one must provide what is missing.

An alchemical poem says:

上德無為入性功，何須修補調虧盈。

"Superior virtue has no doing," and you enter the practice of Xing (Nature):
is there any need of repairing or harmonizing what is damaged or full?[5]

The *Cantong qi* says:

上德無為，不以察求，下德為之，其用不休。

"Superior virtue has no doing":
it does not use examining and seeking.
"Inferior virtue does":
its operation does not rest.[6]

In his commentary to the *Cantong qi*, Liu Yiming (1734–1821) explains this passage as follows:

---

[4] *Daode jing*, 38: "Superior virtue has no doing: there is nothing whereby it does. Inferior virtue does: there is something whereby it does."

[5] In a slightly different form, this poem is found in Liu Qiaoqiao's (1839–1933) *Qiaoqiao dongzhang*.

[6] *Cantong qi*, chapter 7. (References are to Chen Zhixu's redaction.)

修道有二法。一以道全形之事，一以術延命之事。上德者，以道
全其形，抱元守一，行無為之道，即可了事，故曰「上德無為，
不以察求」也。下德者，以術延其命，由勉抵安，行有為之道，
方能還元，故曰「下德為之，其用不休」也。夫上德之所以不察
求者，以其上德之人，天真未傷，客氣未入，若頓悟本性，無修
無證 … 。察求之功無所用。下德之所以用不休者，以其天真已
虧，知識已開，雖能頓悟本性，不能立即馴順，必用漸修之道，
增減之功 … 。此不休之用所由貴也。上德下德，身份不一，故
其用亦異 … 。但終同歸一途。

For the cultivation of the Dao there are two methods: one is the
pursuit of bringing one's form (*xing*) to completion by means of the
Dao, the other is the pursuit of extending one's life (*ming*) by means
of a practice.

Superior virtue brings the form to completion by means of the
Dao. One embraces the Origin and guards Unity, and performs the
way of "non-doing"; thus one can exhaust all pursuits. Therefore
the *Cantong qi* says, "Superior virtue has no doing: it does not use
examining and seeking." Inferior virtue extends life by means of a
practice. One begins from effort and ends with stability, and performs the way of "doing"; thus one is able to revert to the Origin.
Therefore the *Cantong qi* says, "Inferior virtue does: its operation
does not rest."

The reason why superior virtue "does not use examining and
seeking" is that in the person of superior virtue, Celestial Reality (*tianzhen*) has never been damaged and extraneous breaths
(*keqi*) have never entered. Since one immediately awakens to
one's fundamental Nature, there is nothing to cultivate and
nothing to verify. . . . The function of examining and seeking does
not operate.

The reason why the operation of inferior virtue "does not rest" is
that Celestial Reality is lacking and cognition has begun. Although
one could immediately awaken to one's fundamental Nature, one
cannot follow it as is. One must use the way of gradual cultivation
(*jianxiu*) and the function of augmenting and decreasing
(*zengjian*).[7] . . . This is why the unceasing use [of inferior virtue] is
valuable.

---

[7] "Augmenting and decreasing" refers to the cycles of increase and decrease
of Yin and Yang in the Fire Times; see below, pp. 74 ff.

> Superior virtue and inferior virtue are different and are not the same. Therefore their uses are dissimilar. . . . However, they lead to the same goal.[8]

Liu Yiming also says:

> 上德者，行無為之道以了性。下德者，行有為之道以了命。

> Superior virtue performs the way of non-doing and thus fulfills Nature (*liaoxing*). Inferior virtue performs the way of doing and thus fulfills Life (*liaoming*).[9]

Therefore, as we have seen in the Introduction, *Awakening to Reality* emphasizes the progress of the practice saying:

> 始於有作人難見，及至無為眾始知，但見無為為要妙，豈知有作是根基。

> It begins with *doing*, and hardly can one see a thing,
> when it comes to *non-doing*, all begin to understand.
> But if you only see *non-doing* as the essential marvel,
> how can you know that *doing* is the foundation?[10]

Essentially, "superior virtue" refers to the body of childhood, when the precelestial particle of numinous radiance is not yet damaged. Therefore there is no need to perform the practice of "laying the foundations." "Inferior virtue" refers to the body after one's "celestial reality" has been damaged. One should refine oneself using the practice of "laying the foundations," as only thus can the process of aging be inverted and can one return to youth. This is the difference between the practice of Xing (Nature) and the practice of Ming (Life) at the beginning of the practice. This is also why "laying the foundations" is the beginning of "doing" in the alchemical path, and the texts describe it repeatedly.

*Essence, Breath, Spirit.* According to the alchemical texts, Essence, Breath, and Spirit are a single entity, rather than individual "substances" juxtaposed to one another. Nevertheless, as far as the practice is concerned, one is bound to rank them according to their importance, and to arrange them into a sequence. In his *Secret Text of Green Florescence* (*Qinghua biwen*),

---

[8] *Cantong zhizhi,* "Jingwen," chapter 2.
[9] *Cantong zhizhi,* "Jianzhu," chapter 2.
[10] *Wuzhen pian,* "Jueju," poem 42.

19

Zhang Boduan establishes five levels: the Heart (*xin*) is the lord (*jun*); Spirit is the ruler (*zhu*); Breath is the operation (*yong*); Essence comes from Breath; and the Intention (*yi*) is the "go-between" (*mei*). These are their respective functions at the stage of "laying the foundations." In fact, however, both Heart and Spirit pertain to Spirit, and the Intention is the dynamic state (*dongtai*) of Spirit. Therefore, although Zhang Boduan establishes five levels, they actually consist of the "three families" of Essence, Breath, and Spirit. Accordingly, the practice of "laying the foundations" will be described in the present chapter with reference to these three components. First, however, I will provide an explanation of several focal points of the practice.

## 1. Main Points in the Practice of "Laying the Foundations"

### The Opening (qiao 竅)

The first step of the practice is "guarding the Opening" (*shouqiao*). This step is also called "guarding Unity" (*shouyi*) and "guarding the Center" (*shouzhong*). Although these terms have similar meanings, they differ in certain respects. "Guarding Unity" refers to the one point that is guarded in a state of quiescence. "Guarding the Opening" means concentrating one's thoughts on the Opening of the Barrier (*guanqiao*). "Guarding the Center" refers to the center of the body. These three terms, therefore, are not entirely equivalent to one another. In this section, the Opening will be discussed in accordance with Zhang Boduan's *Four Hundred Words on the Golden Elixir*.

As can be expected, the Taoist alchemical texts contain different explanations of the term One Opening of the Mysterious Barrier (*xuanguan yiqiao*), each of which claims to be correct. According to some, this is the "ancestral opening" (*zuqiao*) located between the eyebrows; according to others, it is the Cavity of the Yellow Court (*huangting xue*) located above the navel; according to others, it is the lower Cinnabar Field (*dantian*) located behind the navel; and according to others, this Opening does not exist, in the sense that it has no definite location and is an "empty similitude."[11] Indeed, one should not rigidly adhere to the literal meaning of the terms used in the alchemical methods; a flexible attitude is required to grasp what they hide beneath the surface. Liu Yiming's commentary to *Awakening to Reality* says:

玄關一竅，無方無所，無形無象。

The One Opening of the Mysterious Barrier has no extension, no position, no form, no image.[12]

An anonymous master said:

玄關一竅，重在「一」字，守中抱一，即守一竅也。丹書萬卷，不如守一，能知一，萬事畢。所以此「一」字即注意靜守之處。

In the expression One Opening of the Mysterious Barrier, what is important is the word "One." Guarding the Center and Embracing Unity means guarding the One Opening. In all the ten thousand scrolls of the writings on the Elixir, nothing is more important than guarding Unity. When you are able to comprehend Unity, all pursuits are concluded. Therefore the word "One" refers to what one concentrates on and to what one guards in a state of quiescence.

From this we can deduce that at the stage of "laying the foundations," one guards the lower Cinnabar Field; at the stage of the Barrier of the Hundred Days, one guards both the lower Cinnabar Field and the Emptiness-Rooftop cavity (*xuwei xue*); at the stage of the Barrier of the Ten Months, one guards the middle Cinnabar Field; and at the stage of the Barrier of the Nine Years one guards the upper Cinnabar Field. All these are different forms of "guarding Unity."[13]

*The lower Cinnabar Field.* The lower Cinnabar Field is the Cinnabar Field in the strict sense. Different views exist concerning its position. The medical texts usually say that it is located 1.3 inches below the navel. According to the alchemical texts, instead, it is found 1.3 inches behind the navel. Its

---

[11] The expression "empty similitude" (*xubi*), which occurs frequently in the alchemical texts, derives from the poem of the *Jindan sibai zi* quoted below, p. 84.

[12] *Wuzhen zhizhi*, commentary to "Xutian Xijiang yue."

[13] Barrier of the Hundred Days (*bairi guan*), Barrier of the Ten Months (*shiyue guan*), and Barrier of the Nine Years (*jiunian guan*) refer to the three main stages of the Neidan practice; see below, p. 63. For the Emptiness-Rooftop cavity, see page 33.

location corresponds to the point of intersection of the Thoroughfare and the Girdle vessels (*chongmai* and *daimai*).[14] Since this point, projected onto the external surface of the belly, forms a shape similar to the Chinese character for *tian* 田 ("field"), it is called "Cinnabar Field." Why is it also said that the Cinnabar Field is located 1.3 inches below the navel? Zhao Taiding (Ming dynasty) gives the following explanation:

> 臍下一寸三分者，謂仰臥而取之，入裏又一寸三分為是，是即腎間也。

> When we say 1.3 inches below the navel, this measure is taken with the body lying horizontally. [The Cinnabar Field] then is the point found 1.3 inches under the navel, that is, between the kidneys.[15]

In addition these explanations, there is another one. The Cinnabar Field is where the Elixir coalesces. As this is similar to a seed sown in a field, which naturally gives birth to sprouts and fruits that ripen in due time, it is called "field."

In general, Taoism and medicine agree on one important point with regard to the position of the lower Cinnabar Field: this is the point that directs the functioning of the entire body. Moreover, although the Confucian "quiescence" (*jing*), the Taoist "embracing Unity" (*baoyi*), and the Buddhist "contemplation" (*changuan*) have different names, they all, in fact, seek the stability of the center. This is another point that requires attention.[16]

*The middle Cinnabar Field.* The middle Cinnabar Field is located above the navel. Here the Embryo coalesces in the second stage of the practice,

---

[14] *Chongmai* is also translated as Central vessel or Penetrating vessel. *Daimai* is also translated as Belt vessel.

[15] *Maiwang*, chapter 1.

[16] *Author's note*: In addition to those mentioned above, there are several other views about the position of the lower Cinnabar Field. For example, the *Baopu zi* (chapter 18) says that the lower Cinnabar Field is found two inches below the navel; the central Cinnabar Field is found below the heart; and the upper Cinnabar Field is found above the eyebrows. Another Taoist text says: "In the brain there is the upper Cinnabar Field; it is the palace that stores Spirit. In the Crimson Palace (i.e., the heart) there is the central Cinnabar Field; it is the palace that stores Breath. Three inches below the navel there is the lower Cinnabar Field; it is the palace that stores the Essence." However, since here we are concerned with Zhang Boduan and his *Awakening to Reality*, our discussion is based on his work and on other texts belonging to the Southern Lineage of Neidan.

namely, "refining Breath to transmute it into Spirit." In his *Four Hundred Words on the Golden Elixir*, Zhang Boduan says:

此竅非凡竅，乾坤共合成。名為神氣穴，內有坎離精。

This Opening is not a common opening,
it is formed by the joining of Qian ☰ and Kun ☷.
It is called Cavity of Spirit and Breath,
within are the essences of Kan ☵ and Li ☲.[17]

According to these words, the middle Cinnabar Field is actually the Yellow Court (*huangting*). Why does Zhang Boduan say that "it is formed by the joining of Qian and Kun"? An answer is found in the *Xingming guizhi* (Teachings on the Joint Cultivation of Nature and Life):

天之極上處距地之極下處，相去八萬四千里，而天地之中，適當四萬二千里之中處也。若人身一小天地也，心臍相去亦有八寸四分，而中心適當四寸二分之中處也。

The distance between the highest extremity of Heaven and the lowest extremity of the Earth is 84,000 *li*; therefore the central point is 42,000 *li* away from each of them. Since the human body is a microcosm, the distance between the heart and the navel is 8.4 inches; therefore the central point is 4.2 inches away from each of them.[18]

These words imply that, analogously to the macrocosm, the center of the human microcosm harbors the Opening of the Original Ancestral Breath (*yuanshi zuqi zhi qiao*). Therefore the middle Cinnabar Field is also called Cavity of the Ancestral Breath (*zuqi xue*).

Moreover, in the preface to his *Four Hundred Words on the Golden Elixir*, Zhang Boduan says:

身中一竅，名曰玄牝。此竅者，非心非腎，非口鼻也，非脾胃也，非穀道也，非膀胱也，非丹田也，非泥丸也。能知此之一竅，則冬至在此矣，藥物在此矣，火候亦在此矣，沐浴在此矣，結胎在此矣，脫胎亦在此矣。

---

[17] *Jindan sibai zi*, poem 7.
[18] *Xingming guizhi*, "Heng ji," section 2. Heaven and Earth are equivalent to Qian and Kun, respectively.

> The One Opening at the center of the person is the Mysterious-Female (*xuanpin*). This Opening is not the heart, is not the kidneys, is not the mouth or the nose, is not the spleen or the stomach, is not the anus, is not the bladder, is not the Cinnabar Field, and is not the Muddy Pellet (*niwan*). If one is able to understand this Opening, then the winter solstice, the Medicine, the Fire Times, the "bathing" (*muyu*), the coalescing of the Embryo, and the delivery of the Embryo are all found there.[19]

In this view, the Opening is the Yellow Court. However, the alchemical masters keep this subject secret and do not wish to discuss it in a clear way; they intentionally disclose the various positions of the Opening of the Barrier (*guanqiao*), with the only exception of the Yellow Court. This omission is not accidental; on the contrary, it suggests that the One Opening of the Mysterious-Female is the same as the Yellow Court.[20]

Concerning the Mysterious-Female, *Awakening to Reality* says:

> 要得谷神長不死，須憑玄牝立根基。

> If you want to obtain the Spirit of Valley and live forever,
> you must rely on the Mysterious-Female to establish the
> foundation.[21]

And again:

> 玄牝之門世罕知，休將口鼻妄施為。

> Few in the world know the Gate of the Mysterious-Female:
> stop fiddling around with your mouth and your nose.[22]

In his commentary, Ye Wenshu (twelfth century) writes:

> 玄牝之宮，即中宮也，中藏真一之炁，生金精也。

---

[19] *Jindan sibai zi*, in *Xiuzhen shishu*, chapter 5, preface.

[20] In the Taoist tradition, the Yellow Court is in the first place the center of the human being, in both its physical and non-physical aspects. Other meanings of this term, such as "spleen" (one of the five viscera), are secondary compared to this primary meaning (the spleen, in particular, is the center only when the framework of reference is the five viscera).

[21] *Wuzhen pian*, "Jueju," poem 39. The terms Spirit of the Valley (*gushen*) and Mysterious-Female (*xuanpin*) derive from *Daode jing*, 6.

[22] *Wuzhen pian*, "Jueju," poem 40. The Gate of the Mysterious-Female (*xuanpin zhi men*) is sometimes said to be found in the mouth or the nose.

The Palace of the Mysterious-Female is the Central Palace. It stores the Breath of True Unity, and generates the Essence of Metal.[23]

*The upper Cinnabar Field.* The upper Cinnabar Field, which is located at the top of the head, is also called Palace of the Muddy Pellet (*niwan gong*). Since the body is a microcosm, and the head corresponds to Heaven, the alchemical masters call it Palace of Qian ☰ (*qiangong*), with reference to the trigram that represents Heaven. When the practice reaches the stage of "refining Essence to transmute it into Breath," this Opening is the place where one "reverts the course of the Essence to replenish the brain" (*huanjing bunao*) and "eliminates the ore to keep the gold" (*qukuang liujin*). When it reaches the stage of "refining Breath to transmute it into Spirit," it is the point where the Yang Spirit (*yangshen*) rises.

A poem in *Awakening to Reality* says:

萬卷仙經語總同，金丹只此是根宗，依他坤位生成體，種向乾家交感宮。

The scriptures of the Immortals, ten thousand scrolls,
all tell one thing:
only the Golden Elixir
is the ancestor, the root.
Relying on the other in the position of Kun ☷,
it comes to life and acquires a body,
then it is planted within the house of Qian ☰,
in the Palace of Conjunction.[24]

The *Xingming guizhi* explains this poem as follows:

運北方水中之金，以制南方火中之木，是謂以黑見紅，則凝神入乾頂而成丹。

Circulate the Metal found within the Water in the northern direction, in order to control the Wood found within the Fire in the southern direction. This is called "using the black to see the red."

---

[23] *Wuzhen pian*, in *Xiuzhen shishu*, "Jueju," commentary to poem 39. The Essence of Metal is, ultimately, the Elixir.
[24] *Wuzhen pian*, "Lüshi," poem 16.

Then coagulate your Spirit in the Summit of Qian ☰, and you will achieve the Elixir. [25]

Cui Xifan's *Ruyao jing* (Mirror for Compounding the Medicine) says:

產在坤，種在乾，但至誠，法自然。

It is born in Kun ☷
and is planted in Qian ☰;
as long as you are thoroughly sincere,
the conjunction happens spontaneously.[26]

*Terminology.* Two charts in the *Xingming guizhi* contain lists of synonyms of the three Openings. They mention thirty-four names of the lower Cinnabar Field, including Northern Ocean (*beihai*) and Penghu;[27] fifty-eight names of the middle Cinnabar Field, including Central Yellow (*zhonghuang*) and Center of the Compass (*guizhong*); and forty-eight names of the upper Cinnabar Field, including Purple Prefecture (*zifu*), Celestial Palace (*tiangong*), and Mountain of the Jade Capital (*yujing shan*). These names are originally found in different alchemical texts, and the two charts provides useful materials for their comprehension.[28]

*Awakening to Reality* says:

異名同出少人知，兩者玄玄是要機。

Few people know that they have different names, but come forth together:
both are mystery upon mystery: this is the essential key.[29]

In his commentary to the *Daode jing*, Li Xiyue (1806–56) explains the expression "mystery upon mystery" (*xuanxuan*) saying:

---

[25] *Xingming guizhi*, "Li ji," section 4. Black and red are the colors associated with the North (Water) and the South (Fire), respectively. The Summit of Qian (*qianding*) is the upper Cinnabar Field.

[26] *Ruyao jing*, in *Xiuzhen shishu*, chapter 13.

[27] Penghu is a mythical island in the Eastern Sea, which is a residence of the Immortals.

[28] *Xingming guizhi*, "Pu zhaotu" and "Fan zhaotu."

[29] *Wuzhen pian*, "Jueju," poem 41. These verses allude to *Daode jing*, 1: "These two come forth together but have different names; both are called a mystery. Mystery and then again mystery, gate of all marvels."

「玄之又玄，眾妙之門」系丹家以玄關為有無妙竅。「妙」即無
名之物，故用無欲以靜觀之。「微」即竅，為有名之物，故用有
欲以應觀之。

"Mystery and then again mystery, gate of all wonders." The alchemical masters deem the Mysterious Barrier (*xuanguan*) to be the Wondrous Opening of Being and Non-Being. "Wondrous" is the Nameless; therefore one contemplates it by quiescence and by not having intentions. "Subtle" is the Opening and is the Named; therefore one contemplates it by responding and by having intentions.[30]

In fact, with regard to the "two mysteries" of contemplating the Opening, in a state of quiescence one guards Unity and internally illuminates oneself; in a state of movement, instead, one's Intention (*yi*) leads the cyclical "clearing of the barriers."[31] The Gate of the Mysterious-Female (*xuanpin zhi men*) is where "non-doing" and "doing" respond to one another. This Gate comprises the upper, middle, and lower Cinnabar Fields, and is not an additional opening apart from them.[32]

## The Vessels (mai 脈)

The second step of the practice consists in "clearing the barriers" (*tongguan*). This includes clearing the Function and the Control vessels (*renmai* and *dumai*) and clearing the Eight Vessels (*bamai*).[33] The eight "extraordinary vessels" (*qijing bamai*) are already discussed in the earliest Chinese medical text, the *Lingshu jing* (Book of the Numinous Pivot). Their function in alchemy, however, is clarified by Zhang Boduan.

According to the theory of the conduits described in the medical texts, the human body contains twelve "ordinary channels" (*zhengjing*) and eight "extraordinary channels" (*qijing*), or vessels. Li Shizhen's *Bencao gangmu* (Pharmacopoeia Arranged into Headings and Subheadings)

---

[30] *Daode jing zhushi*, commentary to sec. 1 (the quotation is not literal).

[31] On "clearing of the barriers" (*tongguan*) see the next section of the present chapter.

[32] *Author's note*: See Liu Yiming, *Wuzhen zhizhi*, "Jueju," commentary to poem 40.

[33] *Renmai* is also translated as Conception vessel; *dumai* is also translated as Governor vessel.

includes two chapters entitled "An Investigation of the Eight Extraordinary Vessels" ("Qijing bamai kao"). Under the entry devoted to the Yin Heel vessel, this work quotes Zhang Boduan's *Book of the Eight Vessels* as follows:

八脈者：冲脈在風府穴下；督脈在臍後；任脈在臍前；帶脈在腰；陰蹻脈在尾閭前陰囊下；陽蹻脈在尾閭後二節；陰維脈在頂前一寸三分；陽維脈在頂後一寸三分。凡人有此八脈，俱屬陰神，閉而不開，惟神仙以陽炁冲開，故能得道。八脈者先天大道之根，一炁之祖。採之惟在陰蹻為先，此脈才動，諸脈皆通，次督、任、冲、三脈，總為經脈造化之源。

The Eight Vessels are the Thoroughfare vessel (*chongmai*), found below the cavity of the Wind Palace (*fengfu xue*); the Control vessel (*dumai*), found behind the navel; the Function vessel (*renmai*), found before the navel; the Girdle vessel (*daimai*), found in the waist; the Yin Heel vessel (*yin qiaomai*), found before the Caudal Funnel (i.e., the coccyx) and under the scrotum; the Yang Heel vessel (*yang qiaomai*), found behind the Caudal Funnel, at the second articulation; the Yin Linking vessel (*yin weimai*), found 1.3 inches before the top of the head; and the Yang Linking vessel (*yang weimai*), found 1.3 inches behind the top of the head.

Everyone has these eight vessels. However, since they all pertain to the Yin Spirit (*yinshen*), they are closed. Only the divine immortals are able to open them by infusing them with Yang Breath. By doing so, they obtain the Dao.

The Eight Vessels are the roots of the Great Dao prior to Heaven, and the ancestors of the One Breath (*yiqi*). Among them, one should begin with the Yin Heel vessel, for as soon as this vessel is in movement, all other vessels are cleared. Then one works on the Function, the Control, and the Thoroughfare vessels, because they are the sources of the transformations of all other channels and vessels.[34]

The positions of the Eight Vessels mentioned by Zhang Boduan do not match those given in the medical texts. Nevertheless, Li Shizhen acknowledged that the principles of the alchemical texts should be presented with those of the medical texts, and held Zhang Boduan's views on this matter in high regard.

---

[34] *Bencao gangmu*, "Qijing bamai kao." This and the next quotations from the "Qijing bamai kao" given by Wang Mu are slightly shortened compared to the original text.

*The Function and Control Vessels.* Among the Eight Vessels, the Function and the Control vessels are the most important in the Taoist alchemical practices. According to the alchemical texts, the Control vessel begins in the Caudal Funnel (*weilü*, i.e., the Meeting of Yin cavity, *huiyin xue*), crosses the Spinal Handle (*jiaji*), passes through the Jade Pillow (*yuzhen*), rises to the Muddy Pellet (*niwan*), and terminates at the Mouth Extremity cavity (*duiduan xue*) just above the upper lip. The Function vessel begins in the Meeting of Yin point, rises along the abdomen in the front of the body, and terminates in the Receiver of Fluids cavity (*chengjiang xue*), under the lower lip. Li Shizhen says:

任督二脈，人身之子午也，乃丹家陽火陰符升降之道，坎水離火交媾之鄉。崔希範『天元入藥鏡』云：「歸根竅，復命關，貫尾閭，通泥丸」。俞琰注『參同契』云：「人身血氣，往來循環，晝夜不停」。醫書有任督二脈，人能通此二脈，則萬脈皆通。『黃庭經』言：「皆在心內運天經，晝夜存之自長生」，天經乃吾身之黃道，呼吸往來於此也。鹿運尾閭，能通督脈，龜納鼻息，能通任脈，故二物皆長壽。

The Function and Control vessels are equivalent to Zi (子) and Wu (午) within the human body. In the Way of the Yang Fire and the Yin response of the alchemical masters, which rise and descend [within the body], these vessels are the loci where the Water of Kan ☵ and the Fire of Li ☲ conjoin. Cui Xifan's *Mirror for Compounding the Medicine* says:

> Return to the Root-Opening (*genqiao*),
> revert to the Barrier of Life (*mingguan*),
> pierce through the Caudal Funnel (*weilü*),
> pervade the Muddy Pellet (*niwan*).

In his commentary to the *Cantong qi*, Yu Yan (1258–1314) says: "Within the human body, blood and breath circulate back and forth, all day and all night without pause."[35] The medical texts describe the Function and Control vessels saying that if one is able to clear them, all other vessels are cleared. The *Scripture of the Yellow Court* (*Huangting jing*) says:

---

[35] This sentence is actually found in Yu Yan's *Yiwai biezhuan* (The Separate Transmission of the *Book of Changes*).

They all reside in the heart, and spin the Heaven's Warp;
Maintain them day and night, and you will live for long.[36]

The Heaven's Warp (*tianjing*) is one's own Yellow Path (*huangdao*);[37] inspiration and expiration occur there. When the deer enters the Caudal Funnel, it can clear the Control vessel; when the turtle enters one's breathing, it can clear the Function vessel. Therefore these two creatures confer long life.[38]

Why does Zhang Boduan place the Function and Control vessels before and behind the navel? To elucidate this point, Li Shizhen quotes the explanation given by Wang Haicang (Yuan dynasty):

張平叔言鉛乃北方正氣一點，初生之真陽，為丹母。陽生於子，藏之命門，元氣之所系，出入於此。其用在臍下，為天地之根，玄牝之門。… 升而接離，補而成乾，陰歸陽化，是以還元。

Zhang Boduan says that Lead is the one particle of the Correct Breath of the North, the first-born True Yang that becomes the "mother of the Elixir" (*danmu*). The Yang principle is born from Zi (子) and is stored in the Gate of Life (*mingmen*); what pertains to Original Breath enters and exits from here. Its operation is below the navel: it is the Root of Heaven and Earth, and the Gate of the Mysterious-Female. . . . As it rises, it merges with Li ☲, and by replenishing Li, it forms Qian ☰. The Yin principle returns where it belongs, the Yang principle is transformed, and one reverts to the origin.[39]

This shows that, according to Zhang Boduan, what is found "before the kidneys and behind the navel" is the source of the circulation of Yin and Yang. Through the alchemical practices, the ascent along the Control vessel and the descent along the Function vessel are equivalent to the process of "the Yin principle returning where it belongs, the Yang principle being transformed." Under this respect, there are no major differences between the alchemical and the medical texts.

---

[36] *Huangting neijing jing*, poem 8. In the *Huangting jing*, the subject of this passage is the gods who reside in the human body.

[37] See below, p. 86.

[38] *Bencao gangmu*, "Qijing bamai kao." In the last paragraph, "deer" alludes to the "deer chariot" (see p. 83), and "turtle" alludes to "breathing like a turtle" (*guixi*), an expression equivalent to "breathing through the heels" (see pp. 43 ff.).

[39] *Bencao gangmu*, "Qijing bamai kao."

*Clearing the Function and Control vessels.* At the stage of "laying the founda-tions," one should first clear the Control and Function vessels in order to allow Breath to circulate. However, since the steps of this practice are not always the same, the terminology also differs. At this initial stage, circu-lating Breath along the Function and the Control vessels is called "clear-ing the Function and Control vessels" (*tong rendu*) or "clearing the three Barriers" (*tong sanguan*). Despite the different names, the practice con-sists only in enabling Breath and heat to circulate, in order to open a path for the upcoming refining of the Medicine. In his *Method of Sitting in Quiescence of Master Yinshi* (*Yinshi zi jingzuo fa*), Jiang Weiqiao (1872–1955) relates his personal experiences as follows:

> 在靜坐裏忽感震動，熱氣由尾閭上升頭頂，沿任督循環，復透過頂，自顏面徐徐下降心窩而達於臍下，久之則此動力，自能上下升降，並可以意運之於全身，洋溢四達。

> When I was sitting in quiescence, I suddenly experienced a vibration. A warm energy (*qi*) rose from the Caudal Funnel to the top of my head, circulated through my body along the Function and Control vessels, passed again through the top of my head, and then slowly descended through my chest, until it reached the area below the navel. After some time, this energy began to rise and descend spontaneously. By means of my Intention (*yi*), I could move it throughout the body, so that it permeated my four limbs.

This practice corresponds to clearing the Breath and clearing the vessels.

Physicians maintain that clearing the Function and Control vessels is the Lesser Celestial Circuit (*xiao zhoutian*), and that clearing the Eight Vessels is the Greater Celestial Circuit (*da zhoutian*). From the point of view of the alchemical practice, instead, both of these methods pertain to the initial stage. Therefore the terminology used in the alchemical texts and in present-day Qigong is not the same. For the alchemical texts, in particular, "clearing the Breath" means clearing the Function and Control vessels; "circulating the Medicine" refers to the cycle of the River Chariot (*heche*, i.e., the Lesser Celestial Circuit); and "nourishing the Medicine" refers to the Greater Celestial Circuit. The routes are the same, but the functions are different. Other terms and expressions related to the Barrier of the Hundred Days (*bairi guan*) include "Yang ascends and Yin descends," "advancing the Fire and withdrawing in response" (*jinhuo tuifu*), "turning around the Three Chariots" (*sanche yunzhuan*), "Zhun ䷂ in the morning and Meng ䷃ in the evening," "causing the hexagrams to revolve," and "turning the Wheel of the Dharma."

The goal of the stage of "laying the foundations" is replenishing the shortages in the vital functions of the body. Clearing the Function and Control vessels and clearing the three Barriers consists only in permeating these vessels with "postcelestial breath" (*houtian qi*), which circulates following a cyclical route and makes them clear. It should be noted that at this time the Medicine has not yet been formed: this practice is only done in preparation for the stage of "refining Essence and transmuting it into Breath." Nevertheless, from a medical point of view, the circulation of breath and blood through unobstructed conduits is of great benefit for "nourishing life" (*yangsheng*) and for the treatment of illnesses.

*The Yin Heel or Emptiness-Rooftop cavity.* According to Zhang Boduan, as we have seen above (p. 28), the fulcrum of the Function and Control vessels is in the Yin Heel cavity (*yin qiaoxue*). When the medical texts mention the Yin Heel, they mean a vessel of the Minor Yin (*shaoyin*) channel in the foot. This vessel emerges from the Blazing Valley cavity (*rangu xue*) in the malleolus and rises to the Eyes' Light cavity (*jingming xue*). For the medical texts, therefore, the Yin Heel is not an "opening" (*qiao*). According to the Zhang Boduan, instead, the point in front of the Caudal Funnel is the location of the Meeting of Yin cavity. Therefore in his *Book of the Eight Vessels* he says:

> 陰蹻一脈，其名頗多，曰天根、曰死戶、曰復命關、曰生死竅。
> 上通泥丸，下透湧泉。倘能知此，使真炁聚散，皆從此關竅，則
> 天門常開，地戶永閉。尻脈周流於一身，貫通上下。和炁自然上
> 朝，陽長陰消，水中火發，雪裏花開，所謂「天根月窟閑來往，
> 三十六宮皆是春」。

The Yin Heel vessel has many names: it is called Heaven's Root (*tiangen*), Door of Death (*sihu*), Barrier of the Return to Life (*fuming guan*), and Opening of Life and Death (*shengsi qiao*). Above it communicates with the Muddy Pellet, below it passes through the Bubbling Spring (*yongquan*). If you know this vessel, you will be able to collect and disperse your Breath from the Opening of the Barrier; then the Gate of Heaven (*tianmen*) will be constantly open and the Door of Earth (*dihu*) will be forever closed.

The coccyx vessel runs through the entire body, connecting what is above to what is below. When the harmonious Breath spontaneously pays homage on high, the Yang will grow and the Yin will be extinguished; Water will issue Fire, and a flower will bloom in the snow. This is what is meant by the verses, "Leisurely go back and forth between the Moon's Lair and the Heaven's Root: in all the thirty-six palaces it is spring."[40]

The *Xingming guizhi* clearly arranges these points at the Meeting of Yin cavity, which it calls the Emptiness-Rooftop cavity (*xuwei xue*). It also lists thirty-four synonyms, which include all those mentioned by Zhang Boduan.[41]

During the Qing dynasty, Liu Qiaoqiao (1839–1933) wrote in his *Daoyuan jingwei ge* (Delicate Songs on the Origins in the Dao):

虛危穴，即地戶禁門是也，上道天谷，下達湧泉，真陽初生之時，必由此穴經過，故曰關係最大。昔日呂祖教劉海蟾曰:「水中起火妙在虛危穴」。故海蟾長坐陰蹻，而轉老還童矣。道經認為，人身精炁聚散，水火發端，陰陽交會，子母分胎，均在此處，所以『黃庭經』有「閉塞命門保玉都」之句，玉都即在此穴也。位在任督中間。

The Emptiness-Rooftop cavity is the Forbidden Gate (*jinmen*) of the Door of the Earth. Above it communicates with the Heaven's Valley (*tiangu*), below it reaches the Bubbling Spring (*yongquan*). When the True Yang is just born, it must pass through this cavity; therefore it is said that "it enjoys first-class connections." Anciently, Lü Dongbin gave this teaching to Liu Haichan: "To kindle the Fire within Water, the marvel lies in the Emptiness-Rooftop cavity." Therefore Haichan performed the practices of the Yin Heel, inverted the process of aging, and returned to youth.

According to the Taoist scriptures, in the human body Essence and Breath collect and disperse, Water and Fire come forth, Yin and Yang conjoin, and the Embryo is born: all this occurs at this point (i.e., the Emptiness-Rooftop cavity). Therefore the *Huangting jing* contains the verse, "Close the Gate of Life (*mingmen*) and protect the Jade Capital (*yudu*)." The Jade Capital is this cavity, which is located between the Function and the Control vessels.[42]

---

[40] *Bencao gangmu*, "Qijing bamai kao." The final two verses come from a poem by Shao Yong, quoted below, p. 57.

[41] *Xingming guizhi*, "Fan zhaotu." — *Author's note*: In the human microcosm, the Emptiness-Rooftop cavity corresponds to the lunar mansions Emptiness (*xu*) and Rooftop (*wei*), which in turn represent the joining of the Sun and the Moon.

[42] *Daoyuan jingwei ge*, "Xuanzhu chuanguan ge," section 11. The verse quoted from the *Huangting* is found in the "Inner" version ("Neijing"), poem 35.

*Conclusion.* According to the medical texts, the Function and Control vessels are the two main vessels: the Control vessel is in charge of the Yang vessels, and the Function vessel has control on the Yin vessels. Since they manage all other vessels, once the Function and Control vessels have been cleared, the six other vessels are also progressively cleared. As Yin Zhiping (1169–1251) says in his *Jiqian ge* (Song of Following the Antecedent):

> 一陽動處眾陽來，玄竅開時竅竅開。
>
> Where one Yang moves, all the other Yang arrives;
> when the Mysterious Opening opens, all the other Openings are
>    open.

In fact, these words refer to the clearing of the Eight Vessels.[43]

At this time, the circulation along the Function and Control vessels is nothing more than a route. The ascent and descent of the River Chariot, instead, pertains to the work practice of "refining Essence and transmuting it into Breath." Details on this subject will be found in the next chapter.

## The Three Barriers (sanguan 三關)

In the ascending path along the Control vessel, three points are arduous to overcome. The alchemical texts call them "barriers" (or "passes," *guan*). Xiao Tingzhi (fl. 1260–64), a fifth-generation disciple of Zhang Boduan, wrote in his *Jindan wenda* (Questions and Answers on the Golden Elixir):

> 問背後三關。答曰。腦後曰玉枕關，夾脊曰轆轤關，水火之際曰
> 尾閭關。
>
> Someone asks what are the three Barriers on the back. The one behind the brain is called Barrier of the Jade Pillow (*yuzhen*). The one in the Spinal Handle (*jiaji*) is called Barrier of the Pulley (*lulu*).

---

[43] *Author's note:* According to Li Shizhen, the Mysterious-Female (*xuanpin*) is the same as the Function and Control vessels, but this view is different from the one found in the alchemical texts.

The one at the junction of Water and Fire is called Barrier of the Caudal Funnel (*weilü*).[44]

The Barrier of the Caudal Funnel is located in the lowest section of the spine. The Barrier of the Spinal Handle is in the back, across from the heart. The Barrier of the Jade Pillow is behind the head, below the identically-named acupuncture point, across from the mouth. *Awakening to Reality* contains few references to the three Barriers, because at that time they were the object of oral transmission. However, Xiao Tingzhi was a disciple of Peng Si (fl. 1217–51), and Peng Si received the transmission from Bai Yuchan (1194–1229?), the fifth patriarch of the Southern Lineage. Therefore Zhang Boduan did provide explications on the three Barriers, even though he did not put them in writing and did not explicitly mention them.

In fact, the three Barriers are three sectors of the Control vessel, which forms the first half of the cyclical route of the River Chariot (*heche*) in the alchemical practice. When the circulation of Breath reaches these three points, one frequently encounters obstructions that make it hard to pass through the Barrier of the Jade Pillow. Therefore the *Zhong-Lü chuandao ji* (Records of the Transmission of the Dao from Zhongli Quan to Lü Dongbin), using a metaphor, says that in order to go past this barrier one should use an "ox chariot" (*niuche*).[45] When the constant cycling of the internal Breath reaches the Jade Pillow, one cannot overcome the obstruction unless one proceeds slowly: one can only use the "gentle fire" (*wenhuo*) and the subtle operation of the Intention (*yi*), and should not proceed with strength.

The cyclical path for refining the Elixir is summarized by the expression "three Fields in the front, three Barriers in the back" (*qian santian, hou sanguan*). The ascent in the back is called "advancing the Yang Fire" (*jin yanghuo*), the descent in the front is called "withdrawing by the Yin response" (*tui yinfu*). At the stage of "laying the foundations," one full cycle is called "clearing the Function and Control vessels" (*tong rendu*); after the formation of the Medicine, it is called Lesser Celestial Circuit.[46] The *Huanyuan pian* (Reverting to the Origin), written by Zhang Boduan's disciple, Shi Tai (?–1158), says:

---

[44] *Xiuzhen shishu*, chapter 10.
[45] *Zhong-Lü chuandao ji*, in *Xiuzhen shishu*, chapter 15, "Lun heche." See also below, pp. 83 ff.
[46] On this difference in terminology see below, p. 43.

一孔玄關竅，三關要路頭，忽然輕運動，神水自然流。

The One Opening is the Mysterious Barrier,
the Three Barriers are the essential route.
Suddenly a gentle movement begins,
and the Divine Water spontaneously flows.[47]

In the *Jindan dacheng ji* (The Great Achievement of the Golden Elixir) by Xiao Tingzhi we read:

妙運三田須上下，自知一體合西東，幾回笑指崑山上，夾脊分明有路通。

The wondrous circulation through the Three Fields requires going
　　upward and downward,
and one knows for oneself that East and West join in one body.
Delighted, it moves repeatedly to the summit of Mount Kunlun:
the Spinal Handle is luminous, and the path is open.[48]

Since Shi Tai was Zhang Boduan's main disciple, and Xiao Tingzhi was his fifth-generation disciple, their views on the three Barriers pertain to Zhang Boduan's transmission. The poem by Xiao Tingzhi explains that there is a downward movement in the front of the body through the three Cinnabar Fields, followed by an upward movement along the Control vessel that goes through the Spinal Handle and reaches "Mount Kunlun," i.e., the top of the head, also called Palace of the Muddy Pellet. Poems like the ones quoted above provide more details on this subject.

## 2. The Functions of Essence, Breath, and Spirit

In the whole tradition of *Awakening to Reality*, the material foundation of the Internal Elixir is the Medicine (*yao*). The formation of the Medicine involves Essence, Breath, and Spirit, which the alchemical texts call the Three Treasures. This term refers to the three major components of human life.

---

[47] *Huanyuan pian*, poem 16. (Wang Mu quotes the text from the *Daozang jiyao*. In the *Daozang*, the first line reads: "The One Opening is the Three Barriers.")
[48] *Xiuzhen shishu*, chapter 11, poem 5.

Taoist Internal Alchemy subdivides the refinement of the Three Treasures into several stages. In the first stage, Essence is transmuted into Breath, and Essence and Breath are the refined into Spirit; this is the process of "the Three returning to the Two, and the Two returning to the One." Finally, when the Three Treasures have returned to the One Spirit (*yishen*), Spirit is refined in order to return to Emptiness. The foundation of Taoist inner refining lies, therefore, in the Three Treasures. At the stage of "laying the foundations," the Three Treasures are first replenished; then they become abundant and flourishing; and finally they form the source for the return to a youthful state—the Inner Elixir.

## Spirit (shen 神)

The alchemical texts attach most importance to the refining of Spirit: from "laying the foundations" to "returning to Emptiness," the whole process is ruled by Spirit. A postface to *Awakening to Reality* says: "If you want to embody the supreme Dao, nothing is more important than understanding the Heart. The Heart is the axis of the Dao."[49]

According to Zhang Boduan, Heart and Spirit are related as follows: the Heart is the ultimate foundation, and Spirit is born from the Heart; the foundation of the Heart consists in non-doing and non-movement; as it moves, it is called Spirit. Therefore Zhang Boduan says in his *Secret Text of Green Florescence*:

> 心者，神之舍也。

> The Heart is the residence of Spirit.[50]

He adds:

---

[49] *Wuzhen pian*, in *Xiuzhen shishu*, chapter 30, postface. — Here and elsewhere, the word *xin* is translated as "heart," except when it is juxtaposed to *shen* in the pair "mind and body," or when it refers specifically to the mind as the organ of thought. In all other cases, "mind" would not convey all the nuances and implications of the Chinese term *xin*; in particular, it would obscure the fact that *xin* also means "center—just like "heart" does in English—and refers in the first place to the center of the human being.

[50] *Qinghua biwen*, "Xin wei jun lun."

蓋心者，君之位也。以無為臨之，則其所以動者，元神之性耳。
以有為臨之，則其所以動者，欲念之性耳。

Essentially, the Heart takes the position of the lord. With regard to "non-doing," that through which it moves is the nature of the Original Spirit. With regard to "doing," that through which it moves is thoughts and desires.[51]

These sentences state that Spirit is stored within the Heart. As it moves, it becomes Spirit. Its movement in "non-doing" is called Original Spirit (*yuanshen*), its movement in "doing" is called "cognitive spirit" (*shishen*). Therefore Zhang Boduan also says:

心靜則神全，神全則性現。

When one's Heart is quiescent, one's Spirit is whole. When one's Spirit is whole, one's Nature manifests itself.[52]

Although the concepts behind their names are similar, Heart and Spirit differ in rank and priority. According to Zhang Boduan, the Heart is "silent and unmoving," and the Spirit moves in response to impulses. What Taoism calls "refining Nature" (*lianxing*) is the cultivation of the Heart; what it calls "refining Life" (*lianming*) is the joint cultivation of Essence, Breath, and Spirit. As shown by Chen Tuan's (ca. 920–89) *Wuji tu* (Chart of the Ultimateless), the Ultimateless (*wuji*) is the Heart; the movement of Yang and the quiescence of Yin are the Spirit; and what gathers the five agents together is the Intention (*yi*). Therefore Chen Tuan also upholds the view that "Spirit is the ruler."

According to the alchemical methods of Zhang Boduan, "refining Ming (Life)" comes first, and "refining Xing (Nature)" comes later. At the initial stage of "laying the foundations," however, Xing and Ming are cultivated together: since the practice at this stage consists in replenishing one's Ming and in cultivating the ultimate foundation, both Xing and Ming should be attended to simultaneously. Therefore the initial stage involves collecting the mind (*shouxin*), guarding Unity (*shouyi*), ceasing thoughts (*zhinian*), and entering the state of quiescence (*rujing*). These four expressions show that, at this stage, one should perform practices to eliminate the impure thoughts (*zanian*). The *Secret Text of Green Florescence* says in this concern:

[51] *Qinghua biwen*, "Shen wei zhu lun."
[52] *Qinghua biwen*, "Xin wei jun lun."

38

但於一念妄生之際，思平日心不得靜者，此為梗耳。急捨之，久久純熟。夫妄念莫大於喜怒，怒裏回思則不怒，喜中知抑則不喜，種種皆然，久而自靜。

When even one thought arisen due to delusion is sufficient to cause continuous mental activity, so that the Heart cannot be quiescent, this is a cause of hindrances. Rapidly dismiss that thought; in due course you will become skilled in doing this. Now, among deluded thoughts none is of greater import than joy or anger. If, when you experience anger, you are able to recollect, then you will not experience anger. If, when you experience joy, you know how to restrain it, then you will not experience joy. If you do this every time, eventually you will attain quiescence.[53]

This passage refers to ending the flow of thoughts. Therefore collecting the mind is the first requirement to enter the state of quiescence and to control the inner Heart, keeping it silent and unmoving. Although impure thoughts may arise, they are at once restrained. This is the first practice.

"Embracing Unity" means concentrating the mind on one point in order to remove the impure thoughts. Here the word "unity" is meant in a broad sense, i.e., collecting the Heart and the Spirit in one point. Guarding the Cinnabar Field and guarding the "ancestral opening" (zuqiao)[54] can attain the goal of collecting the mind and ceasing thoughts.[55]

Inner observation (neishi) is also a method of collecting the mind. The *Secret Text of Green Florescence* says:

心之所以不能靜者，不可純謂之心。蓋神亦役心，心亦役神，二者交相役，而欲念生焉。心求靜，必先制眼。眼者神遊之宅也，神遊於眼而役於心。故抑之於眼而使之歸於心。

When the Heart cannot be quiescent, this is not simply due to the Heart itself. Essentially, Spirit makes use of the Heart, and the Heart

---

[53] *Qinghua biwen*, "Xin wei jun lun."

[54] On the "ancestral opening" see above, p. 20.

[55] *Author's note*: In its discussion of "guarding the Center" and "embracing Unity," the *Xingming guizhi* considers that there are a center with a fixed position as well as a center without a fixed position. The center with a fixed position is the Cavity of the Yellow Court (huangting xue). The center without a fixed position is the noumenal Center in which Heaven and Earth dwell together, i.e., the Center of the Heart. Embracing Unity means guarding that one place. The *Xingming guizhi* says: "Embracing Unity is the same as guarding the Center of that Unity." In other words, this means guarding in quiescence any of the Openings.

makes use of Spirit. They make use of one another, and because of this, thoughts and desires are born. If the Heart seeks quiescence, it is first of all necessary to control the eyes. The eyes are the residences for the roaming of Spirit: Spirit roams through the eyes, and makes use of the Heart. Therefore restrain Spirit through the eyes and cause it to return to the Heart.[56]

According to the principles of Taoist alchemy, Spirit is stored in the Heart and is issued from the eyes. In the practice of inner observation, the emphasis is on "observation": when the eyes are used to observe inwardly, one's thinking becomes focused, and the Original Breath surges; one internally illuminates oneself, all concerns become empty, delusive thoughts vanish, and one's Heart is calm and untroubled. This is the third step for entering the state of quiescence. An anonymous master said:

天之神發於日，人之神發於目，目之所至，心亦至焉。

The Spirit of Heaven is issued from the Sun, the Spirit of Man is issued from the eyes. Wherever the eyes go, the Heart also goes.

Therefore when the alchemical masters sit to practice, they coagulate Spirit and stabilize breathing, press the tongue lightly against the upper palate, concentrate the Heart and the eyes inwardly, look down at their Cinnabar Field, and can rapidly enter the state of quiescence.

*Intention.* The *Secret Text of Green Florescence* also says: "Intention is the go-between."[57] The Intention (*yi*) is the operation of Spirit; the so-called True Intention (*zhenyi*) means that the thought activity issues from the Spirit. If we identify the mind with the brain, then the function of the brain is the Spirit, and its thinking faculty is the Intention. If one controls the joining of the Three Treasures by means of the Intention, then one can activate its intermediary function among the Three Treasures.

For this reason, the Intention is also called "go-between" and Intention-Soil (*yitu*). The meaning of "go-between" is that it introduces Yin and Yang to one another for their conjunction. Therefore the alchemical texts also call it Yellow Dame (*huangpo*): "yellow" indicates that it pertains to the central agent Soil, and "dame" means that it is the "matchmaker" (*meipo*), a metaphor for the intermediary that allows the joining of Yin and Yang.

---

[56] *Qinghua biwen*, "Xin wei jun lun."
[57] *Qinghua biwen*, "Yi wei mei shuo."

*Awakening to Reality* attributes a great importance to the Intention-Soil, considering that the True Intention operates throughout the entire alchemical process: Metal, Wood, Water, and Fire achieve completion by means of the True Intention (*zhenyi*). One of its poems says: "The four images and the five agents all avail themselves of Soil."[58] Liu Yiming explains that the "four images" are the Breaths of Metal, Wood, Water, and Fire; with Soil, these are the five agents (*wuxing*). Soil, which stands for the Intention (*yi*), harmonizes the four Breaths; it forms one "family" by itself, and is the Golden Elixir.

According to the principles of alchemy, Fire in the first place is a code name of the Spirit; since Wood generates Fire, Wood stands for the Original Spirit, and Fire stands for the postcelestial Spirit. Analogously, Water is a code name of the Essence; since Metal generates Water, Metal stands for the Original Essence, and Water stands for the postcelestial Essence. Metal and Water form one family; Wood and Fire form one family; and Soil on its own forms one family. *Awakening to Reality* says:

三五一都三箇字，古今明者實然稀，東三南二同成五，北一西方四共之。戊己身居生數五，三家相見結嬰兒，嬰兒是一含真氣，十月胎圓入聖基。

Three, Five, One —
all is in these three words;
but truly rare are those who understand them
in past and present times.
East is 3, South is 2,
together they make 5;
North is 1, West is 4,
they are the same.

Wu (戊) and Ji (己) dwell on their own,
their birth number is 5;
when the three families see one another,
the Infant coalesces.
The Infant is the One
holding True Breath;
in ten months the embryo is complete —
this is the foundation for entering sainthood.[59]

[58] *Wuzhen pian*, "Lüshi," poem 11.
[59] *Wuzhen pian*, "Lüshi," poem 14.

"Three, Five, One" means that the three "fives" return to the One.

At the stage of "laying the foundations," guarding the Cinnabar Field is called "guarding the Intention": one's True Intention (*zhenyi*) is placed within the Cinnabar Field. When clearing the Function and Control vessels, guarding the Cinnabar Field is called "being guided by the Intention": Intention (*yi*) guides the Breath, and the Breath journeys through the Function and Control vessels. When one enters the state of quiescence, it is said that "the Intention follows the turning of Breath": here it is important that one "neither forgets nor assists," and is "neither tense nor inert." All this pertains to the operation of the True Intention (*zhenyi*).

The True Intention (*zhenyi*) has different functions at each of the three stages of the alchemical practice. The present section has been concerned with its operation and meaning at the stage of "laying the foundations." The more advanced meanings will be examined in the following chapters.

## Breath (qi 氣)

In the alchemical practice, Breath has a wide meaning: it involves both the breath of respiration and the precelestial Breath, or internal Breath (*neiqi*). Refining Breath is an important component of the stage of "laying the foundations."

At the beginning of the practices of collecting the mind and ceasing thoughts, one performs the ordinary breathing: exhaling, the belly contracts; inhaling, it expands. This is called "harmonizing the breathing" (*tiaoxi*). Although there are many methods of "harmonizing the breathing," their common goal is leading one to enter the state of quiescence. Before clearing the Function and Control vessels, one should progressively shift to "inverted breathing": exhaling, the belly expands; inhaling, it contracts. The technical term for this is "practice of the bellows" (*tuoyue gongfu*).

When, in the next stage of the practice, the inhaled breath rises along the Control vessel and the exhaled breath descends along the Function vessel, inhaling and exhaling must join one another. Unless one is already accustomed to inverted breathing, one cannot practice the circulation of the River Chariot. In the alchemical texts, this is called "harmonizing the true breathing" (*tiao zhenxi*).

An an even more advanced stage, one does not rely on inhaling and exhaling. At that stage, the spontaneous circulation of the internal Breath (*neiqi*) is called "circulation of the hidden Breath" (*qianqi yunxing*). It should be noted that, in present-day Qigong, the "circulation of the hidden Breath" is called Lesser Celestial Circuit, but the alchemical texts use the latter term with a different meaning.[60]

When the preliminary practices of "laying the foundations" have reached the stage of replenishing the Essence, the gradual coagulation of Spirit, Breath, and Essence occurs. Later, after the Medicine is generated, it is refined together with Spirit. To refer to Breath at this stage of the practice, the Longmen masters use the character 「炁」(pronounced *qi*) instead of the standard character 「氣」(also pronounced *qi*). This character is used as a code name for the joining of Essence and Breath.

The alchemical texts usually make a distinction between "respiration" (*huxi*, lit., "exhaling and inhaling") and "harmonizing the breathing" (*tiaoxi*). In the latter term, the primary meaning of the word *xi* 息 is "exhaling and inhaling." However, when the alchemical texts use this word, they intend to point out the difference between two kinds of breathing. The *Zhuangzi* says:

> 真人之息以踵，眾人之息以喉。

> The True Man breaths through the heels, the common man breaths through the throat.[61]

A gloss on this passage says: "'Heels' means that inhalation and exhalation reach the Bubbling Spring" (*yongquan*).[62] The *Zhuangzi* editor, Guo Qingfan (1844–96), notes: "'Breathing through the heels' means that the breathing is extremely deep. This shows that the True Man is in a state of deep quiescence." The *Xingming guizhi* provides further explanations:

> 一切常人呼吸皆隨咽喉而下，至中脘而回，不能與祖氣相連，如魚飲水而口進腮出，即莊子所謂「眾人之息以喉」是也。如是至人呼吸則直貫明堂，而上至夾脊，而流入命門，得與祖氣相連，

---

[60] In Neidan, the Lesser Celestial Circuit is the route of the River Chariot (*heche*); see pp. 71 ff.

[61] *Zhuangzi*, chapter 6 ("Da zongshi").

[62] The Bubbling Spring (*yongquan*) is located on the soles of the feet.

如磁吸鐵，而同類相親，即莊子所謂「真人之息以踵」是也。踵者，真息深深之意。

The common people's breathing always begins from the throat and then descends, reaches the stomach and then turns around. Thus their breath cannot join the Ancestral Breath; it is like a fish drinking water, which enters from the mouth and exists from the cheeks. This is what Zhuangzi meant when he said, "The common man breaths through the throat." The breathing of the man of attainment, instead, passes through the Hall of Lights (*mingtang*), rises to the Spinal Handle, and flows into the Gate of Life. There it can join with the Ancestral Breath. It is like magnetite attracting iron, or like things of the same kind that join with one another. This is what Zhuangzi meant when he said, "The True Man breaths through the heels." "Heels" means that his breathing is extremely deep.[3]

According to the *Zhuangzi*, therefore, the True Man's "breathing through the heels" refers to the precelestial Breath, i.e., the "circulation of the hidden Breath" that we have mentioned above. The common people, instead, breath through the throat, and this is the respiration based on the postcelestial breath. If one focuses on the precelestial Breath, allowing it to rise from the Bubbling Spring, ascend through the Spinal Handle, surge to the Muddy Pellet, descend to the lower Cinnabar Field, and join with the postcelestial breath, then the two breaths join as one, and inhalation and exhalation become extremely deep. This is what Cui Xifan meant when he wrote in his *Ruyao jing*:

> 先天炁，後天氣，得之者，常似醉。
>
> Breath prior to Heaven,
> breath posterior to Heaven —
> those who obtain them
> always seem drunk.[4]

This "Breath prior to Heaven" (*xiantian qi*) is the Breath that pervades the Eight Vessels.

"*Embryonic breathing.*" Although the *Zhuangzi* distinguishes "breathing through the throat," or *houxi*, from "breathing through the heels," or *zhongxi*, in both cases the word *xi* 息 means "inhalation and exhalation."

---

[3]  *Xingming guizhi*, "Heng ji," section 1.
[4]  *Ruyao jing*, in *Xiuzhen shishu*, chapter 13.

When the later alchemical texts use this word, instead, they often mean the internal breathing, i.e., the "circulation of the hidden Breath." For example, the term "embryonic breathing" (*taixi*) means that Breath has reached a stage in which the breathing through the nostrils is extremely subtle and almost imperceptible, as if the external inhaling and exhaling had come to a halt. The Eight Vessels are cleared, and the whole body feels comfortable; just like an embryo in the womb, there is no external inhaling and exhaling, but only the "circulation of the hidden Breath." This state, nevertheless, pertains to the initial stage of the practice, when the harmonization of breathing serves to pacify the Heart. When the practice progresses, and Heart and Spirit become one, then Heart and breathing rely on one another, and one reaches the state in which one forgets one's self. Then, by means of the practice of quiescence, the External Medicine is spontaneously produced, and the stage of "laying the foundations" is concluded.

*Awakening to Reality* says:

> 謾守藥爐看火候，但安神息任天然。

> Desist from guarding the furnace of the Medicine
> and from watching over the fire times:
> just settle the breathing of the Spirit
> and rely on the celestial spontaneity.[65]

This means that one can refine the Medicine only after the "breathing of the Spirit" has settled. This state, however, can only be sought by means of such practices as the "breathing through the heels" and the "embryonic breathing."

The *Taixi ming* (Inscription on Embryonic Breathing), which is appended to one of the editions of the *Taixi jing* (Scripture of Embryonic Breathing) in the Taoist Canon, says:

> 三十六咽，一咽為先，吐唯細細，納唯綿綿。坐臥亦爾，行立坦然 … 假名胎息，實曰內丹，非只治病，決定延年。

> As regards the thirty-six breathings, for each of them the most important thing is that exhalation should be very slight, and inhalation should be very long drawn. Whether sitting or lying, this rule should be observed; whether walking of lying, the breathing should be smooth. . . . This is metaphorically called "embryonic breathing";

---

[65] *Wuzhen pian*, "Lüshi," poem 13.

in fact, it is the Internal Elixir. Not only will it cure diseases: it will also grant a long life.[66]

The *Taixi jing* itself says:

心不動念，無來無去，不出不入，自然常住。

If the Heart does not stir thoughts, neither coming nor going, neither exiting nor entering, it will constantly dwell of its own accord.[67]

These passages refer to the actual practice of "embryonic breathing."

## Essence (jing 精)

In the alchemical texts, Essence, Breath, and Spirit are specialized terms, used in substantially different ways compared to the medical texts. These differences are often indicated by the use of such expressions as Original Essence (*yuanjing*), precelestial Essence (*xiantian jing*), or True Essence (*zhenjing*), on the one hand; and postcelestial essence (*houtian jing*) or "essence of the intercourse" (*jiaogan jing*, i.e., semen), on the other hand. Bai Yuchan explicates this point saying:

其精不是交感精，乃是玉皇口中涎。

This essence is not the essence of the intercourse: it is the saliva in the mouth of the Jade Sovereign.[68]

The Jade Sovereign (Yuhuang) represents the Origin, and the "saliva in his mouth" represents the precelestial state. This passage shows that the terms used in the alchemical texts should not be confused with those used in the medical texts. Min Yide's (1748–1836) commentary on this passage states: "This is what we call Original Essence."

When the alchemical texts use the word "original" (*yuan*), they refer to the Origin (*yuanshi*), i.e., to a primordial substance that is not born in

---

[66] *Taixi jing zhu*, "Taixi ming."
[67] *Taixi jing zhu*.
[68] *Shangqing ji*, in *Xiuzhen shishu*, j. 39.

the postcelestial state. Therefore the *Shihan ji* (Records from a Stone Casket), attributed to Xu Jingyang (also known as Xu Xun, trad. 239–374), says:

> 元陽即元精，發生於玄玄之際。元精無形，寓於元炁之中。若受外感而動，與元炁分判，則成凡精。
>
> Original Yang is the same as Original Essence, sent forth from the bourns of the Mystery beyond the Mystery. Original Essence has no form, and resides within Original Breath. If it receives an external stimulus, then it moves: it separates from Original Breath, and becomes the common essence.[69]

During the Ming dynasty, Wan Shangfu wrote:

> 精在先天時，藏於五臟六腑，氤氳而未成形，後天之念一動，則成為後天之精。
>
> When the Essence is in the precelestial state, it is stored in the five viscera and the six receptacles, misty and murky and still formless. As soon as a single thought moves in the postcelestial state, it becomes the essence of the postcelestial state.[70]

This shows that, in the alchemical texts, the word "essence" denotes the life functions and the very foundation of life, in a way comparable to the internal secretions and the hormones.

Taoism deems Essence to be the "mother of the Elixir" (*dammu*) and regards it as life's basic element. When the Essence is damaged, it causes weakening and aging; when it is reborn, it can lead to a long life. A flourishing energy is the foundation of youthful vigor. When this basic element coagulates with Breath, the Elixir is achieved. If the code name "essence" found in the alchemical texts is confused with the physiological essence discussed in the medical texts, misunderstandings can easily occur.

*Essence as "prima materia."* Wu Shouyang (1574–1644) says in his *Xian Fo hezong yulu* (Recorded Sayings on the Common Origin of the Immortals and the Buddhas):

---

[69] *Shihan ji*, chapter 1 (the quotation is not literal).
[70] Wan Shangfu, *Tingxin zhai kewen*.

元精何故號先天，非象非形未判乾。太極靜純如有動，仙機靈竅
在無前。

Why is the Original Essence called "precelestial"?
The undivided Qian ☰ is devoid of image and form.
In the Great Ultimate, quiescent and pure, there is something like a
    movement:
The Numinous Opening, mainspring of immortality, lies in what has
    nothing prior to Itself.[71]

This poem requires an explanation.[72] Qian ☰ stands for Heaven. "Undivided Qian" means the time when Heaven and Earth have not yet separated from one another and are in an inchoate state; they are devoid of form and image, and there is only the Breath of Emptiness and Non-Being. These sentences describe Original Essence as the earliest stage in the origin of the cosmos. This Essence blooms into the misty and murky Great Breath, and lodges within the five viscera: it is not the physiological essence of the medical texts.

The Great Ultimate is Emptiness and Non-Being; it is "ultimate emptiness" and "utmost quiescence."[73] Within the precelestial Original Essence, after "guarding Unity" and "harmonizing the breathing," quiescence reaches a state of ultimate purity. Then there is the subtle awareness of a movement: the Medicine is going to be generated. The word "like" in the sentence "there is something like a movement" means that it seems to be a movement, but actually is not a movement. This Essence is entirely devoid of the qualities of the postcelestial essence, and thus can be used as *prima materia* (*yuanliao*) to compound the Numinous Medicine (*lingyao*).

"The Numinous Opening, mainspring of immortality" is that in which "there is something like a movement." In the expression "lies in what has nothing prior to Itself," "nothing" (*wu*) means that there is not yet matter: as it "lies in what has nothing prior to Itself," it is devoid of form and matter. Breath is exceedingly abundant and Essence is exceedingly pure: this is the nature of the precelestial Essence, or Original Essence.

---

[71] *Xian Fo hezong yulu*, "Ji Wang Zhu Taihe shijiu wen," no. 3.

[72] The explanation given by Wang Mu is based on the comments made by Wu Shouyang on his own poem quoted above.

[73] These expressions are drawn from *Daode jing*, 16: "Attain ultimate emptiness, guard utmost quiescence."

Although Wu Shouyang was a master of the Northern Lineage, he lived at the end of the Ming period and thus he could also receive the transmission of the Southern Lineage. The understanding of the Original Essence after the unification of the two lineages is the same.

*The nature of Original Essence.* The Essence, Breath, and Spirit that are used for compounding the Elixir are, in the first place, a single entity, and cannot be sharply distinguished from one another. However, the stage of "laying the foundations" consists of practices of replenishment. Since Essence is the foundation of the Elixir, Spirit is the ruler, and Breath is the moving force, what needs to be replenished at this stage is most often the Original Essence. Therefore protecting, replenishing, and harmonizing the Essence have the purpose of improving the foundation. Essence, Breath, and Spirit then harmonize, transform, and coagulate with one another. When Essence is abundant, Breath is full, and Spirit is flourishing, one can begin the practice of "refining Essence to transmute it into Breath."

In his *Secret Text of Green Florescence*, Zhang Boduan states that Essence comes from Breath. He says:

神有元神，氣有元氣，精得無元精乎？ ⋯ 元神見而元氣生，元氣生則元精產。

As regards Spirit, there is an Original Spirit, and as regards Breath, there is an Original Breath. Therefore as regards Essence, how could there not be an Original Essence? . . . When the Original Spirit appears, the Original Breath is generated, and when the Original Breath is generated, the Original Essence is born.[74]

This is in agreement with Wu Shouyang's discourse quoted above: "The undivided Qian ☰ is devoid of image and form" means that, in the realm of Original Spirit, "there is something like a movement" within the pure and quiescent Great Ultimate, and the Original Breath is generated. "The Numinous Opening, mainspring of immortality, lies in what has nothing prior to Itself" means the time when the Original Essence is born. In the same text, however, Zhang Boduan also says:

藥不離精、氣、神，藥材又精氣神之所產也。 ⋯ 三者孰為重？曰：神為重。金丹之道，始然以神而用精、氣也。〔神氣精常相

---

[74] *Qinghua biwen,* "Jing cong qi shuo."

戀‧而〕神者性之別名也，至靜之餘，元氣方產之際，神亦欲
出，急庸定以待之，不然，是散而無用之體也。

> The Great Medicine cannot separate itself from Essence, Breath,
> and Spirit; and the ingredients of the Medicine are also born from
> Essence, Breath, and Spirit. . . . Which of these three is most
> important? Spirit is most important. The Way of the Golden Elixir
> begins with Spirit, but also uses Essence and Breath. [Spirit,
> Breath, and Essence always long for one another, but] Spirit is
> another name for one's Nature. In the state of absolute quies-
> cence, when the Original Breath is on the point of being
> produced, Spirit is also ready to emerge. You should rapidly
> attend to them, otherwise Spirit would disperse itself and would
> become a useless thing.[75]

This means that the Medicine is formed by the union of "these three." If
any of them is not sufficient, then the stage of "laying the foundation"
has not yet been completed: they cannot be used to make the Numinous
Medicine (lingyao), and without ingredients one cannot "refine Essence
and transmute it into Breath."

Therefore one of Zhang Boduan's poems says:

> 咽津納氣是人行，有藥方能造化生，鼎內若無真種子，猶將水火
> 煮空鐺。

> Swallowing saliva and ingesting breath are human actions;
> only when you have the Medicine can you form and transform.
> If in the tripod there is no True Seed,
> it is like using water and fire to boil an empty pot.[76]

The dregs of the postcelestial state cannot generate the perfectly numinous, precelestial Elixir. This is why Zhang Boduan uses the expression
"true seed" (zhen zhongzi): he emphasizes that he means something
different from a material entity, so that no one would misunderstand his
words.

*Awakening to Reality* also says:

> 見之不可用，用之不可見。

---

[75] *Qinghua biwen*, "Zonglun jindan zhi yao."
[76] *Wuzhen pian*, "Jueju," poem 5.

> What you see cannot be used,
> what you use cannot be seen.[77]

These words clarify that Original Essence is devoid of form and matter. As soon as matter is generated, it cannot be used as "mother of the Elixir." Lü Dongbin says:

> 息精息氣養精神，精養丹田氣養身，有人學得這般術，便是長生不死人。

> Increase your Essence, increase your Breath, and nourish Essence
>      and Breath:
> when your Essence nourishes the Cinnabar Field, your Breath
>      nourishes you.
> Anyone who is capable of studying this Art
> will live a long life without death.[78]

These words clarify, in turn, that Essence, Breath, and Spirit must be refined together.

In the *Huangdi neijing* (Inner Canon of the Yellow Emperor) we read:

> 知之則強，不知則老，故同出而名異耳。智者察同，愚者察異，愚者不足，智者有餘。有餘而耳目聰明，身體輕強，老者復壯，壯者益治。是以聖人為無為之事，樂恬淡之能。

> One who knows them becomes strong, one who does not know them
> becomes old. "They come forth together, but have different
> names."[79] The wise observes their sameness, the foolish observes
> their differences. The foolish does not have enough, the wise has
> more than enough. Since he has more than enough, his ears and
> eyes are sharp and bright, and his body is light and strong; when he
> becomes old he can revert to his prime, and when he is in his prime
> he can benefit the government. Therefore the sage does the deed of
> non-doing and rejoices in the capacity of being calm and tranquil.[80]

---

[77] *Wuzhen pian*, "Wuyan lüshi."

[78] *Quan Tang shi*, chapter 888.

[79] This sentence is quoted from *Daode jing*, 1.

[80] *Huangdi neijing suwen*, "Jingui zhenyan lun." For the last sentence, see *Daode jing*, 2: "The saint dwells in the deed of non-doing," and *Daode jing*, 31: "Calm and tranquility are the best." See also *Zhuangzi*, chapter 15: "Calm and tranquility, silence, emptiness, non-doing: these are the level of Heaven and Earth, the

"The wise observes their sameness" means that Essence, Breath, and Spirit are a single entity, and operate with one another. The transformation of the three is achieved by means of the transformation of Breath in the human body. Therefore Zhang Boduan states in his *Secret Text of Green Florescence* that "Essence comes from Breath." He states, in other words, that at the stage of "laying the foundations" one should refine the Three Treasures together; only then can the Medicine be obtained, and only then can one possess the proper foundation to enter the stage of the Barrier of the Hundred Days.

### 3. Terms Related to the "Coagulation of the Three Treasures"

#### *"Refining"* (lian 煉)

The term "refining" derives from Waidan (External Alchemy). In Waidan, the ingredients are refined by fire. In Neidan (Internal Alchemy), instead, Essence (*jing*) is refined by Spirit (*shen*). Therefore Spirit is represented by Fire, and Essence is represented by Water. "Refining Water by means of Fire" is equivalent to saying that Spirit leads Breath and refines the Essence.

The word "refining" applies to all four stages of the alchemical practice: "laying the foundations," "refining Essence to transmute it into Breath," "refining Breath to transmute it into Spirit," and "refining Spirit to return to Emptiness." In this section, however, I will discuss "refining" only in relation to "laying the foundations."

In Waidan, the basic meaning of the word *lian* (煉) is "to refine by heating." Neidan borrows this word as a metaphor for self-cultivation. After the human body has gone past the age of childhood, Essence, Breath, and Spirit are damaged; therefore they should be replenished before one can start compounding the Medicine. Although the refining of Spirit pertains to the practice of Xing (Nature), and the refining of Essence and Breath pertains to the practice of Ming (Life), at the initial stage of the practice, Xing and Ming should be cultivated together.

substance of the Way and its Virtue." — The reference to "being of benefit to the government" is owed to the fact that, according to tradition, the *Huangdi neijing* was taught to the Yellow Emperor, the first mythical ruler of Chinese history.

Refining the Spirit is the same as refining the Heart. Lü Dongbin says in the *Changdao zhenyan* (True Words Chanting the Dao):

煉丹先要煉心。煉心之法，以去閑思妄想為清靜法門。

Before you refine the Elixir, you must refine your Heart. The method of refining the Heart is the dharma-gate (*famen*) to clarity and quiescence (*qingjing*), through the elimination of idle thoughts and deceiving concepts.[81]

These words highlight the practice of "sitting in quiescence" (*jingzuo*). Bai Yuchan said:

夫道以無心為體，忘言為用，柔弱為本，清靜為基。

The Dao takes having no-mind as the substance, forgetting words as the operation, being yielding and weak as the root, and being clear and quiescent as the foundation.[82]

In his *Secret Text of Green Florescence*, Zhang Boduan says:

心和則氣和，氣和則形和，形和則天地之和應矣。

When the Heart is harmonious, Breath is harmonious; when Breath is harmonious, the form is harmonious; when the form is harmonious, Heaven and Earth respond with their harmony.

Then he continues by saying that seeking the harmony of the Heart lies in the single word "quiescence." If, on seeing or hearing something, one does not experience joy or anger, one can bring one's Heart to quiescence. Zhang Boduan concludes by saying:

口訣曰：目不亂視，神返於心，神返於心，乃靜之本。

The oral instructions say: When the eyes do not see in a disordered way, Spirit returns to the Heart. When Spirit returns to the Heart, this is the foundation of quiescence.[83]

---

[81] *Changdao zhenyan*, chapter 1.

[82] This sentence is found in Ma Danyang's *Danyang zhenren yulu*. It is attributed to Bai Yuchan in the *Changsheng quanjing*. The first two expressions ("having no-mind" and "forgetting words") are drawn from the *Zhuangzi*, and the other two (being "yielding and weak" and being "clear and quiescent") from the *Daode jing*.

[83] *Qinghua biwen*, "Xin wei jun lun."

Here Zhang Boduan maintains that collecting the Heart and the Breath is the focal point of the initial stage of the practice. This is in agreement with the methods of the Northern Lineage (Beizong).

When the Heart is calm, the Breath is harmonious; therefore refining the Spirit is the same as refining the Breath. Refining the Breath, in turn, is equivalent to refining the Spirit: each supports and completes the other, and each is the operation of the other. The practice of "harmonizing the breathing" that we have discussed in one of the previous sections consists in refining the Breath, and corresponds to the teaching found in the poem of *Awakening to Reality* quoted above: "Just settle the breathing of the Spirit and rely on the celestial spontaneity."[84]

With regard to "laying the foundations," the Southern Lineage differs from the Northern Lineage in the emphasis placed on harmonizing, replenishing, and refining the Original Essence. Its masters maintain that, while the state of strength or weakness differs from person to person, in all cases after childhood the Original Essence is subjected to damage. Therefore it should be furthered by means of practices of harmonization. Only then can Original Essence be replenished and become the "mother of the Elixir" (*danmu*). What is the Original Essence? It is the source of the flourishing life force (*shengming li*), the dynamism of incipience and youth; it is related to the vital functions and the internal secretions (*fenbi*). When it is harmonized and replenished by means of the alchemical process, then Essence is abundant, Breath is full, and Spirit flourishes. The Three Treasures coagulate with one another and form the Medicine, and one begins the practices of the Barrier of the Hundred Days.

"*Refining the Ji-Soil.*" In Chinese, "laying the foundations" is also called *lianji* (炼己). The word *lian*, as we have seen, means "to refine." The word *ji* is interpreted in two ways. According to the first interpretation, it means "self" (*ziji* 自己), and *lianji* means to refine one's own Three Treasures in order to build a proper foundation. According to the second interpretation, *ji* means the "Ji-Soil" (*ji-tu* 己土); since Ji 己 is contained within the trigram Li ☲, it means the Original Spirit (also called Nature of the Mind, *xinxing*, and True Intention, *zhenyi*).[85] The *Xingming guizhi* says:

---

[84] *Wuzhen pian*, "Lüshi," poem 13.
[85] *Ji* 己 is the female aspect of Unity, corresponding to the Yin line found within the Yang trigram Li ☲. *Wu* 戊, analogously, is its male aspect, corresponding to the inner line of Kan ☵.

煉己土者，得離日之汞，煉戊土者，得坎月之鉛。戊土上行，己
土下降。

By refining the Ji-Soil (*ji-tu* 己土) you obtain the Mercury within Li ☲, the Sun. By refining the Wu-Soil (*wu-tu* 戊土) you obtain the Lead within Kan ☵, the Moon. The Ji-Soil rises, the Wu-Soil descends.[86]

The technical terms for this practice are "drifting Wu 戊 to reach Ji 己" (*liu wu jiu ji*) and "taking from Kan ☵ in order to fill Li ☲" (*qu kan tian li*). Others call it "using the kidneys to replenish the heart" (*yishen buxin*), "reverting the course of the Essence to replenish the brain" (*huanjing bunao*), or in other ways. Although different authors use these expressions in different ways, they all agree in emphasizing that harmonization and refining constitute the initial stage of the practice.

*Awakening to Reality* says:

離坎若還無戊己，雖含四象不成丹。

If Li ☲ and Kan ☵ do not return to Wu and Ji,
they may well hold the four emblems, but will not make the Elixir.[87]

These verses also refer to the practice of *lianji* (煉己).

## *"Harmonization"* (tiao 調)

The Chinese character 「調」 has two readings and two meanings. When it is read *tiao*, it means "to harmonize, to regulate, to make even." When it is read *diao*, it means "to transfer, to allocate." The alchemical texts contain examples of both usages. Here, however, I will discuss only the first meaning.

"Harmonizing the Spirit" (*tiaoshen*), "harmonizing the breathing" (*tiaoxi*), and "harmonizing the Essence" (*tiaojing*) are actually one and the same thing; even though they are discussed separately, their goal is the same.

---

[86] *Xingming guizhi*, Preface.
[87] *Wuzhen pian*, "Jueju," poem 14. Li is Fire and contains Wood, Kan is Water and contains Metal, but their joining can only occur by means of Soil (Ji and Wu).

*Harmonizing the Spirit.* In his *Secret Text of Green Florescence* (*Qinghua biwen*), Zhang Boduan discusses "harmonizing the Spirit," and maintains that it requires the use of the internal senses of sight, hearing, and smell. His reasoning is as follows:

> 夫兩目為役神之捨，顧瞻視聽，神常不得離之。兩耳為送神之地，蓋百里之音聞於耳，而神隨之而去。兩鼻為勞神之位，隨感而辯辯之者誰？神也。… 〔所以〕忘於目，則神歸於鼎，而燭於內，蓋綿綿若存之時，目垂而下顧也。忘於耳，則神歸於鼎，而聞於內，蓋綿綿若存之時，耳內聽於下也。忘於鼻，則神歸於鼎，而吸於內，蓋真息既定之時，氣歸元海也。

The eyes are the locus for making use of the Spirit. When anything is seen or watched by the eyes, the Spirit cannot separate from it. The ears are the site for sending off Spirit. One might say that if the ears hear a sound coming from one hundred miles away, the Spirit would follow it and would leave. The nostrils are the position for toiling the Spirit. What is it that discriminates following the external impulses? It is the Spirit. . . .

[Therefore] if one detaches oneself from the eyes, then the Spirit returns to the Tripod and the eyes watch inwardly. Essentially, when this becomes "unceasing and continuous," the eyes see what lies below.[88]

If one detaches oneself from the ears, then the Spirit returns to the Tripod and the ears listen inwardly. Essentially, when this becomes "unceasing and continuous," the ears innerly hear what lies below.

If one detaches oneself from the nostrils, then the Spirit returns to the Tripod and one inhales inwardly. Essentially, when this becomes "unceasing and continuous," one's breath returns to the Original Ocean.[89]

Zhang Boduan also says:

> 意生於心，心生於目，故老子曰：「吾嘗觀心，得道亦至矓」。夫真息既定，內光乃神光，此心乃真心。真心生意，神光燭心。故常為之説曰：「目視心，心生意，意採鉛」。

---

[88] The expression "unceasing and continuous" (*mianmian ruocun*) derives from *Daode jing*, 6: "The Spirit of the Valley never dies: it is called the Mysterious-Female. The gate of the Mysterious-Female is called the root of Heaven and Earth. It is unceasing and continuous, and its operation never wears out."

[89] *Qinghua biwen*, "Zhenxie tianji tulun."

The Intention is generated in the Heart, and the Heart is generated in the eyes. Therefore Laozi said: "I always contemplate the Heart, and attain the Dao in the blink of an eye." After the true breathing has been stabilized, the inner radiance is the radiance of the Spirit, and this Heart is the True Heart. The True Heart generates the Intention, and the radiance of the Spirit illuminates the Heart. Therefore it is often said: "The eyes watch the Heart, the Heart generates the Intention, the Intention collects the Lead."[90]

The *Yinfu jing* (Scripture of the Hidden Agreement) says: "The mainspring is in the eyes."[91] Essentially, the Spirit is stored within the Heart and is issued from the eyes. If the Spirit is collected within, then it ties itself to the eyes and one observes inwardly. Thus the Spirit and the eyes contemplate and comprehend together. The "six thieves" (*liuzei*) are removed, leading one to enter a state of quiescence.[92] This is called "circulating the light and inverting the radiance" (*huiguang fanzhao*), "cessation and contemplation" (*zhiguan*),[93] or "inner observation" (*neishi*).

Shao Yong (1012–77) also emphasizes that "harmonizing the Spirit" should be assisted and guided by means of the eyes' "inner observation." In one of his poems he says:

乾遇巽時觀月窟，地逢雷處見天根，天根月窟閑來往，三十六宮皆是春。

When Qian (Heaven ☰) meets Xun (Wind ☴), contemplate the
    Moon's Lair,
when the Earth (Kun ☷) comes across the Thunder (Zhen ☳),
    observe the Heaven's Root.
Leisurely go back and forth between the Moon's Lair and the
    Heaven's Root:
in all the thirty-six palaces it is spring.[94]

According to representation of the human body by means of the trigrams, the top of the head is Qian ☰ (Heaven) and the belly is Kun ☷ (Earth). When the circulation of the internal Breath (*neiqi*) reaches the top of the head, represented by the hexagram Gou ䷫ formed by Heaven ☰ and

---

[90] *Qinghua biwen*, "Caiqu tulun."

[91] *Yinfu jing*, part 3.

[92] The "six thieves" are, in Buddhism, the five sense organs (eyes, ears, nose, tongue, and skin) and the mind.

[93] *Zhiguan* corresponds to Buddhist *śamatha* and *vipaśyanā*.

[94] Shao Yong, *Guanwu jin* (Chant on the Contemplation of Things).

Wind ☴, one guards the Cavity of the Moon's Lair (*yueku xue*), i.e., the "ancestral opening."[95] When it reaches the hexagram Fu ䷗, formed by Earth ☷ and Thunder ☳, one guards the Heaven's Root (*tiangen*), i.e., the Cavity of the Caudal Funnel. Whether one "contemplates" or "observes," in either case one should use the eyes. When the Heart and the eyes operate together, Spirit and Breath join as one.[96] Above one contemplates the Moon's Lair, below one observes the Heaven's Root; the internal Breath moves cyclically, passing through the three Barriers and flowing through the three Fields. All this happens by means of "harmonizing the Spirit."

According to the oral instructions found in the alchemical texts, "at the beginning of the practice one should coagulate the Spirit." In the *Secret Text of Green Florescence*, Zhang Boduan explains:

> 所謂「凝神」者，蓋息念而返神於心，⋯ 神融於精氣也。

> What we call "coagulation of the Spirit" essentially consists in ceasing thought and returning the Spirit to the Heart. . . . This means that Spirit merges with Essence and Breath.[97]

The conjunction of Spirit with Breath and Essence is the benefit of "harmonizing the Spirit." *Awakening to Reality* says:

> 虛心實腹義俱深，只為虛心要識心。

> Empty the mind, fill the belly: the meanings are both profound.
> It is precisely in order to empty the mind that you should know the mind.[98]

Liu Yiming explains this poem saying:

> 虛心者，虛人心，修性之事。實腹者，實道心，修命之事。

---

[95] On the "ancestral opening see above, p. 20.

[96] This sentence is translated as literally as possible. The Chinese text is 「心目同用，神氣合一」.

[97] *Qinghua biwen*, "Jing shen lun."

[98] *Wuzhen pian*, "Jueju," poem 9. The first line of this poem derives from *Daode jing*, 3: "Thus the saint in his government empties the people's minds and fills their bellies."

"Emptying the mind" means emptying the human mind (renxin) and cultivating one's Nature. "Filling the belly" means filling the mind of the Dao (daoxin) and cultivating one's Life.[99]

The terms "human mind" and "mind of the Dao" indicate that during the process of refining one's thoughts into Original Spirit, both Spirit and cognition are functions of the method of harmonization.

*Harmonizing the Breathing.* The functions of "harmonizing the breathing" and "harmonizing the Spirit" are the same. In the *Secret Text of Green Florescence* we read:

> 盖心始欲静而欲念未息。欲念者，氣質之性所為也。 … 其所以役神者，以外物诱之耳。〔故〕静坐之際，先行閉息之道。閉息者，夫人之息一息未際，而一息續之。今則一息既生，而抑後息。後息受抑　，故續之緩緩焉。久而息定。抑息千萬不可動心，動心則逐於息，息未止而心已動矣。 … 〔所以〕閉息而又存心，則心不動，而息亦息矣。

> Essentially, the Heart in the first place wants quiescence, but thoughts and desires do not rest. Thoughts and desires are created by one's temperament (qizhi zhi xing). . . . The Heart makes use of Spirit by enticing it through the external objects. [Therefore] when you are sitting in quiescence, you should first of all practice the method of stopping breathing (bixi).

> What is "stopping breathing"? In the breathing of the common people, before one breath has been completed, it is followed by the next breath. Now, instead, after one breath is born, you restrain the next breath. Since the next breath is restrained, it follows the previous breath unhurriedly. In due time, the breathing becomes stabilized.

> When you restrain your breathing, you should not by any means move your mind: if you move your mind, then it would be chased by your breathing, and before one breath comes to an end, your mind would be already in motion. . . . [Thus] when stop your breathing, and you also maintain your mind quiescent, then your mind does not move, and your breathing rests.[100]

In this passage, Zhang Boduan describes "harmonizing the breathing" as the support to enter the state of quiescence. The later Neidan masters

---

[99] *Wuzhen zhizhi*, "Jueju," commentary to poem 9.
[100] *Qinghua biwen*, "Xiashou gongfu."

called this "internal breathing" (*nei huxi*). This term means that, in inhaling and exhaling through the nose, one's breathing should be subtle and long-drawn, continuous and uninterrupted.

In the *Zhixuan pian* (Pointing to the Mystery), Lü Dongbin says:

但能息息常相顧，換盡形骸玉液流。

If you can let each breath attend to the next breath,
you will transfigure your corporeal shape and the Golden Liquor will
flow.

*Harmonizing the Essence.* An alchemical text explains "harmonizing the Essence" saying:

積神生氣，積氣生精，此自無而至有也。煉精化氣，煉氣化神，
煉神還虛，此自有而至無也。

Accumulating the Spirit to generate Breath, and accumulating the Breath to generate Essence: this is going from Non-Being to Being. Refining the Essence to transmute it into Breath, refining the Breath to transmute it into Spirit, and refining the Spirit to return to Emptiness: this is going from Being to Non-Being.[101]

Therefore Spirit, Breath, and Essence give birth to and form one another, and cannot be separated from each other. When the Spirit in the Heart is harmonized, then Essence is generated. *Awakening to Reality* says:

竹破還應竹補宜，抱雞當用卵為之，萬般非類徒勞力，爭得真鉛
合聖機。

When bamboo breaks, you should use bamboo to repair it;
to hatch a chicken, you must use an egg.
If all things are not of the same kind, you merely toil yourself:
strive to obtain the True Lead, and you will join with the mainspring
of sainthood.[102]

At the stage of "laying the foundations," emphasis is placed on replenishing the Three Treasures. Among them, the Original Essence is the foundation for refining the Elixir; therefore it should be generated and replenished. When it has been replenished, emphasis is placed on "harmoniza-

---

[101] Huang Baijia (1643–1709), *Neijia quanfa*.
[102] *Wuzhen pian*, "Jueju," poem 8.

tion." But how should Original Essence be harmonized? Obviously, by means of one's own vital functions, in order to recover a youthful state. Therefore Zhang Boduan underlines that when bamboo breaks, it should be repaired with bamboo.[103] In his *Huanyuan pian* (Reverting to the Origin), Shi Tai similarly writes:

> 屋破修容易，藥枯生不難，但知歸復法，金寶積如山。

> If the Chamber breaks, repairing it is easy,
> if the Medicine withers, generating it is not difficult.
> As long as you know the method for returning,
> the golden treasure accumulates like a mountain.[104]

The "method for returning" mentioned in this poem is the method of harmonization. In his *Xian Fo hezong yulu* (Recorded Sayings on the Common Origin of the Immortals and the Buddhas), Wu Shouyang says:

> 唯自家以此精補精，以此炁補炁，不必別行異術，何其易修。

> Simply repair by yourself this Essence with your Essence, and this Breath with your Breath. You do not need to perform any odd practice, or how could self-cultivation be easy?[105]

The *Xingming guizhi* says:

> 一者，有物混成，先天地生是也。以其流行謂之炁，以其凝聚謂之精，以其妙用謂之神。始因太極一判，分居陰陽二體之中。是以聖人明天地之要，知變化之源，取精於水府，召神於靈闕，使歸玄牝竅中，三家聚會，合為一體。

> Unity is "something inchoate and yet accomplished, born before Heaven and Earth."[106] As it flows into movement, it is called Breath; as it coagulates and condenses itself, it is called Essence; as it has a wondrous operation, it is called Spirit. Since the division of the Great Ultimate, it resides in the two bodies of Yin and Yang. Therefore the saint comprehends the essentials of Heaven and Earth, and knows the source of all transformations. He collects the Essence from the Palace of Water (*shuifu*), summons the Spirit from the

---

[103] Note that the Chinese word for "repair" and "replenish" is the same, i.e., *bu* 補.

[104] *Huanyuan pian*, poem 60. The "chamber" is the Tripod.

[105] *Xian Fo hezong yulu*, "Wu Taiyi shijiu wen," no. 1.

[106] *Daode jing*, 25.

Numinous Portal (*lingque*), and causes them to return to the Opening of the Mysterious-Female. When the three families coalesce with one another, they join in one body.[107]

According to the passages quoted above, "harmonizing the Essence" requires the joint refining of Essence, Breath, and Spirit; it does not consist in the cultivation of a single entity. Therefore *Awakening to Reality* cautions:

> 陽裏陰精質不剛，獨修此物轉羸尪，勞形按引皆非道，服氣餐霞總是狂。舉世謾求鉛汞伏，何時得見龍虎降，勸君窮取生身處，返本還元是藥王。

> The Yin essence within Yang
> is not a firm substance:
> if you cultivate only this thing
> you will become ever more weak.
> Toiling one's body and pressing and pulling
> is certainly not the Way,
> ingesting breath and swallowing mist
> is entirely foolish.

> The whole world recklessly tries
> to subdue Lead and Mercury —
> when will they be able to see
> Dragon and Tiger submitted?
> I exhort you to probe and grasp
> the place where one comes to life:
> return to the fundament, revert to the origin,
> and you are a Medicine King.[108]

This shows that Original Essence, Original Breath, and Original Spirit cannot be separated from one another, and should be cultivated together. In his commentary to this poem, Liu Yiming says:

> 勞形按引，服氣餐霞，不是煉陰精便是補陰精，與道相隔，愈修愈遠，安能伏真鉛真汞而歸於一氣耶！

> Toiling one's body, pressing and pulling (*anyin*), ingesting breath, and swallowing mist (*canxia*): all this consists either in cultivating

---

[107] *Xingming guizhi*, "Heng ji," section 2.
[108] *Wuzhen pian*, "Lüshi," poem 9.

the Yin essence or in replenishing the Yin essence.[109] This is unrelated to the Dao: the more one would cultivate oneself, the more one would go away from the Dao. How could one subdue the True Lead and the True Mercury, and return to the One Breath?[110]

This passage sheds light on an essential point concerning the three methods of harmonization that we have discussed above.

## 4. Conclusion of the Stage of "Laying the Foundations"

The alchemical practice is divided into two main parts. "Laying the foundations" is the initial practice of replenishing, the preparatory practice for refining the Elixir. The alchemical texts call this stage the "arts of the Way" (*daoshu*). The next three stages, namely the Barrier of the Hundred Days (*bairi guan*, i.e., "refining Essence and transmuting it into Breath"), the Barrier of the Ten Months (*shiyue guan*, i.e., "refining Breath to transmute it into Spirit"), and the Barrier of the Nine Years (*jiunian guan*, i.e., "refining Spirit to return to Emptiness"), are called the "arts of Immortality" (*xianshu*).

When Essence is abundant, when Breath is full, and when Spirit is flourishing, they are called "the three wholes" (*sanquan*). The abundance of Essence is seen in the teeth; the fullness of Breath is seen in the voice; and the flourishing of Spirit is seen in the eyes. After the completion of "laying the foundations," one's teeth are healthy, one's voice is vibrant, one's eyes are luminous, and one can reach the goal of eliminating illnesses and extending the length of life. In fact, the practice at this stage consist in actualizing the inherent life force of the body and in applying the natural, spontaneous potential of the human being. When the mind is in command of the physical body, and the faculty of thought is in control of the nervous system, it is possible to eliminate illnesses and extend one's longevity.

[109] *Anyin* ("pressing and pulling") is a shortened form of *anmo daoyin* (lit., "pressing and rubbing" and "guiding and pulling"). *Daoyin* is a form of gymnastics based on postures that favor the circulation of breaths and essences found within the body. *Anmo* is usually rendered as "massage." "Swallowing mist" (*canxia*) is often mentioned together with "ingesting breath" (*fuqi*) and with "drinking dew" (*yinlu*).

[110] *Wuzhen zhizhi*, "Lüshi," commentary to poem 9.

Several present-day varieties of Qigong applied to medical treatment derive from the initial stage of the alchemical practice. According to Zhang Boduan, however, this stage of the practice should be transmitted by a master. In his *Awakening to Reality* he does not provide detailed indications about this stage, and in his three other works it is seen only sporadically. For this reason, the chapter on "laying the foundations" of the present book has not quoted only poems and passages from *Awakening to Reality*, but also from other sources.

## 2 Refining Essence

## to Transmute it into Breath

In the Taoist alchemical practices of Nourishing Life, the stage of "refining Essence to transmute it into Breath" has a crucial importance, as it represents the first level after "laying the foundations." Building on the basis established in the previous stage, one advances in the work of refining Essence, Breath, and Spirit.

At this stage, Essence, Breath, and Spirit—the Three Treasures—are said to be the ingredients. The practice of "laying the foundations" is intended to replenish their supply. This initial, preparatory practice is called the stage of the "arts of the Way" (*daoshu*). Only after the Three Treasures have been replenished can one enter the stages of refining the Internal Elixir. These stages are called "arts of Immortality" (*xianshu*).

One of the representative sayings concerning "laying the foundations" is: "When Essence is full, one does not think of desires; when Breath is full, one does not think of food; when Spirit is full, one does not think of sleep." This, however, is only an abstraction. The alchemical masters give directions to their disciples by examining their eyes, their teeth, and their voice in order to establish the most fruitful procedure. Another saying refers to this by these words: "When Spirit is abundant, it is shown by the light of the eyes; when Breath is abundant, it is shown by the voice; when Essence is abundant, it is shown by the teeth."

It is said, moreover, that when the Cinnabar Field is as firm as a stone; when one's pace is as light as flying; and when, each time one begins to practice, the "source of the Medicine" is lively and brisk, the "celestial mechanism" is unobstructed and flourishing, and the "substance of Water" is clear and true—when all this happens, one has begun the work of "refining Essence and transmuting it into Breath."

"Refining Essence to transmute it into Breath" is also called the Barrier of the Hundred Days (*bairi guan*). This is only a conventional term, and does not mean that this stage necessarily requires one hundred days.

Since this is a higher stage compared to "laying the foundations," we must explicate several new technical terms in addition to those mentioned in the previous chapter. These explications are meant to provide a general outline of this stage of the practice.

## The Medicine (yao 藥)

What the alchemical texts call the Medicine is made of the Essence, the Breath, and the Spirit that have been replenished at the stage of "laying the foundations." As we have seen, the three ingredients are also called "the three wholes" (*sanquan*). An alchemical text refers to them when it says: "In order for the Great Elixir not to vanish, you need the three wholes. If it requires arduous practice and is hard to achieve, you should blame the evil causes."[1]

According to the different stages of the alchemical practice, the Medicine is divided into three types: the External Medicine (*waiyao*), the Internal Medicine (*neiyao*), and the Great Medicine (*dayao*). This distinction is based on the process of coagulating Essence, Breath, and Spirit with one another. The cyclical refining at the stage of "refining Essence to transmute it into Breath" leads to the formation of the External Medicine. The cyclical refining that follows the completion of the first stage of the practice results in the formation of the Internal Medicine. After the External and the Internal Medicines coagulate with one another, one enters the stage of "refining Breath to transmute it into Spirit," which is called the Great Medicine. After the Great Medicine goes through the barrier of "entering the enclosure" (*ruhuan*, also known as the "barrier of sitting," *zuoguan*), it is called the Embryo of the Dao (*daotai*), or the Infant (*ying'er*).[2]

The "arts of the Way and the "arts of Immortality" differ according to whether, during the circulation along the Celestial Circuit of the

---

[1]  These words seem to be found for the first time in chapter 39 of the *Xiyou ji* (Journey to the West), a novel containing many alchemical allegories.

[2]  On "entering the enclosure" see below, p. 69.

Function and Control vessels, the Medicine has not yet been formed or has already been formed. "Laying the foundations" is the stage in which there is no Medicine, and it only consists in refining Breath. "Refining Essence to transmute it into Breath," instead, is the state in which the formation of the Medicine occurs.

*External Medicine, Internal Medicine, and Great Medicine.* The process of attaining the Medicine involves two "births" and two "collections." The two births are those of the External Medicine and the Internal Medicine. The two collections are those of the External Medicine and the Internal Medicine. The difference between them lies in the fact that for the External Medicine there is a "birth" followed by a "collection," while for the Internal Medicine there is a "collection" followed by a "birth."

This point requires a detailed explanation. When the External Medicine is born—i.e., from the "living Zi hour" (*huo zishi*) onward—Essence, Breath, and Spirit begin to move.[3] The source is clear, and the Original Essence is full. At that time, by means of the Fire Times of the Lesser Celestial Circuit, the Medicine rises to the Muddy Pellet, descends through the trachea, passes through the Yellow Court, enters the lower Cinnabar Field, and is stored there. This counts as one cycle of refining the Medicine. Since it comes from outside and enters within, it is called External Medicine. According to the rule, the External Medicine must be submitted to three hundred full cycles in order to be in accord with the "mysterious and wondrous mechanism" (*xuanmiao ji*). Only then is it possible to begin the alchemical practice to generate the Internal Medicine.

After the preliminary coagulation of the External Medicine has been completed, it rapidly gives birth to the Internal Medicine. One first circulates the Original Spirit, and joins it in the lower Cinnabar Field with the Original Breath already accumulated there by means of the three hundred cycles of refining. This generates the Internal Medicine, which is finer and purer than the External Medicine. However, as we have said, for the Internal Medicine there is a "collection" followed by a "birth." Unlike the External Medicine, the Internal Medicine is not formed by a process of coagulation: this is an immediate method (*dunfa*) belonging to the "arts of Immortality." After the Internal Medicine is born in the lower Cinnabar Field, it is joined to the External Medicine already produced, and they gradually coalesce with one another. This is why it is said that there is a

---

[3] On the "living Zi hour" see below, pp. 106 ff.

"collection" followed by a "birth." The Internal Medicine, therefore, does not use the circulation along the Celestial Circuit; after it is born it meets the External Medicine and they coalesce into the "mother of the Elixir" (*danmu*).

An alchemical text says:

> 外藥所以了命，內藥所以了性。外藥者外奪造化，以復先天；內藥者內保本真，以化後天。...先天真陽，從虛無中來，乃屬於彼，故謂外藥。先天既來，歸根復命，即屬於我，故謂內藥。

> The External Medicine fulfills Life (*liaoming*); the Internal Medicine fulfills Nature (*liaoxing*). The External Medicine "steals creation and transformation" outside, in order to return to the precelestial; the Internal Medicine protects the fundamental reality within, in order to transform the postcelestial. . . .

> The precelestial True Yang comes from Emptiness and Non-Being. As this pertains to the "other" (*bi*), it is called External Medicine. After the precelestial has come, one "reverts to the root and returns to life." As this pertains to the "self" (*wo*), it is called Internal Medicine.[4]

The External Medicine pertains to "doing" (*youzuo*) and is refined by means of the Lesser Celestial Circuit. The Internal Medicine, instead, pertains to "non-doing" (*wuwei*): after one extinguishes the Fire, Spirit enters the Cinnabar Field, joins the External Medicine stored there, and the Internal Medicine is achieved. The entrance of Spirit in the Cinnabar Field is the so-called "collecting" (*cai*), and is also referred to as "coagulating Spirit and letting it enter the Cavity of Breath (*qixue*)." As we have said, one does not use the Celestial Circuit.

The Great Medicine, instead, is refined by means of the Greater Celestial Circuit, i.e., by means of the Original Spirit, which is silent and luminous; but here, in fact, there is no actual "circulation." Since this concerns the stage of "refining Breath to transmute it into Spirit," it will not be described in detail in the present chapter.

*Awakening to Reality* says:

[4] Liu Yiming, *Cantong zhizhi*, "Jingwen," chapter 2. The expression "stealing creation and transformation" (*duo zaohua*) derives from the *Ruyao jing* (Mirror for Compounding the Medicine). The expression "reverting to the root and returning to life" (*guigen fuming*) derives from the *Daode jing*, 16.

內藥還同外藥，內通外亦須通，丹頭和合類相同，溫養兩般作用。

The Internal Medicine is after all the same as the External Medicine;
when the Internal is mastered, the External is mastered too.
In compounding the matrix of the Elixir, the kinds should be the
    same;
"nourishing warmly" requires two kinds of operation.[5]

This poem refers to the process of coagulation and coalescence of the External and the Internal Medicines.

After the Internal and the External Medicines coagulate with one another, there is the sign of the "three appearances of the Yang radiance" (*yangguang sanxian*). Then one can extinguish the Fire and prepare oneself for the seven days of "entering the enclosure" (*ruhuan*).[6] The "mother of the Elixir," obtained by the coagulation of the Internal and the External Medicines, is refined in order to form the Great Medicine, and one enters the next stage, "refining Breath to transmute it into Spirit."

The coagulation of the Internal and the External Medicines with one another is equivalent to the Medicine formed by the coalescence of Essence, Breath, and Spirit. The technical term for this is "Breath" (*qi* 炁). As we have seen, the alchemical texts use the word *qi* 炁 as a code name to mean that the coagulation has been achieved. The "Breath" obtained by "refining Essence and transmuting it into Breath" is the goal of this stage of the practice.

## Transmutation (hua 化)

After Essence, Breath, and Spirit coagulate with one another and form the Medicine, the practice of harmonization allows the Essence to collect

---

[5]  *Wuzhen pian*, "Xijiang yue," poem 1. "Matrix of the Elixir" (*dantou*) is a synonym of "mother of the Elixir" (*danmu*).

[6]  This term appears to derive from, or be related to, the Quanzhen meditation practice of retirement in the *huandu*, "enclosure," which originally lasted one hundred days or three years, and later was performed for shorter periods. The Quanzhen retirement in the *huandu* in turn bears analogies with the Buddhist practice of *biguan*, or "confinement" in a solitary cell. See also below, p. 100.

itself and rapidly produce the "mother of the Elixir" (*danmu*). The process of further sublimation through which the "mother of the Elixir" becomes the material foundation of one's inner refinement is called "transmutation."

Since "refining Essence and transmuting it into Breath" is a stage of replenishment, preliminary to compounding the Medicine, it consists in a process of restoration of the bodily functions. The stage subsequent to the formation of the Medicine, instead, is one of application and operation, and consists in the development of health and vigor. "Transmutation" is the Taoist idea of "the Three returning to the Two, the Two returning to the One, and the One returning to Non-Being."

According to the principles of Taoist alchemy, the alchemical Medicine is made of the Three Treasures, i.e., Essence, Breath, and Spirit. Essence is the foundation of the Three Treasures. Although Original Essence (*yuanjing*) pertains to the precelestial state, it takes on various impurities and becomes a material entity, and cannot ascend to the Muddy Pellet following the spinal column, i.e., the route of the River Chariot. Therefore it must be refined with Breath, and transformed into a "Breath" made by joining Essence and Breath to one another. Being light and pure, and devoid of matter, the Essence can finally circulate following the route of the River Chariot. This is the process of "joining the Three into the Two," also called "refining Essence and transmuting it into Breath." Then the two other components, Spirit and Breath, form the Great Medicine.

At the next stage, "refining Breath to transmute it into Spirit," the word "transmutation" has the same meaning. When Breath is transmuted and returns to being comprised within Spirit, and thus to being one with Spirit, it forms the Embryo of Sainthood (*shengtai*), which is the Elixir. This is the process of entering from Being into Non-Being (*you you ru wu*).

The third and last stage of refining is "refining Spirit to return to Emptiness." Here the word "transmutation" is not used anymore; it is replaced by "return" (*huan*), which means reverting to the Ultimateless.

In his commentary to the *Cantong qi*, Zhu Yuanyu (fl. 1657–69) writes:

凡陰陽對待，一往一來，俱謂之化。神則渾然在中，寂然不動也。

Yin and Yang always attend upon one another. Their coming and going is called "transmutation." The inchoate Spirit is at their center, silent and unmoving.[7]

## *The River Chariot* (heche 河車)

As we have seen in the previous chapter, Zhang Boduan's *Book of the Eight Vessels* describes in detail the Function and Control vessels.[8] When the Control vessel—which runs from the Caudal Funnel to the Muddy Pellet—is used to circulate the Medicine, the alchemical texts refer to it as the route of the River Chariot. The Caudal Funnel, the Spinal Handle, and the Jade Pillow are the "three Barriers" that mark its ascending route. The Muddy Pellet, the Yellow Court, and the lower Cinnabar Field are the three Cinnabar Fields that mark its descending route. The ascent is called "advancing the Fire" (*jinhuo*); the descent is called "withdrawing in response" (*tuifu*). Since the two paths form a circle, the alchemical texts use the term Lesser Celestial Circuit.

*Awakening to Reality* refers to this stage of the practice by saying:

> 河車不敢暫留停，運入崑崙峰頂。
>
> The River Chariot dares not stop for one moment,
> as it enters the summit of Mount Kunlun.[9]

Concerning the purpose of the circulation of the River Chariot, Zhang Boduan says in one of the heptasyllabic poems appended to his *Four Hundred Words on the Golden Elixir*:

> 鵲橋有路透玄關，立鼎安爐自不難，四象合和憑藉土，三花會聚
> 返還山。子初運入崑崙去，午後周流滄海間，更待玉壺點化後，
> 頂門進出換仙顏。
>
> The Magpie Bridge in its route passes through the Mysterious
> Barrier;

[7] *Cantong qi chanyou*, "Riyue hanfu" (section 3).
[8] See above, pp. 28 ff.
[9] *Wuzhen pian*, "Xijiang yue," poem 5.

establishing the tripod and setting up the stove is not hard.
The conjunction of the four images relies on Soil,
the three flowers gather together and return to the mountain.
At Zi (子) they first enter Mount Kunlun, and then leave;
at Wu (午) afterward they flow into the Azure Sea.
Wait for the transmutation in the Jade Pot:
it will exit the gate of the sinciput and take the semblance of an
    Immortal.[10]

This poem describes in detail the path of the circulation of the River Chariot, as well as its results. The term Magpie Bridge (*queqiao*) derives from Cui Xifan's *Ruyao jing*:

上鵲橋，下鵲橋，天應星，地應潮。

The upper Magpie Bridge,
the lower Magpie Bridge:
in Heaven they respond to the stars,
on Earth they respond to the tides.[11]

According to Xiao Tingzhi, a second-generation disciple of Bai Yuchan, the upper Magpie Bridge is the tongue, and the lower Magpie Bridge is in the Yin Heel cavity (*yin qiaoxue*). These two "bridges" connect the paths of the Function and Control vessels to one another. The time of Zi 子 is a metaphor for the time of the initial movement, the kindling of the Fire from the Yin Heel cavity. The time of Wu 午 is a metaphor for the time in which the Medicine reaches the top of the head.[12] After this, the Medicine is delivered to the lower Cinnabar Field. Mount Kunlun is a metaphor for the Muddy Pellet, and the Azure Sea (*canghai*) is a metaphor for the lower Cinnabar Field. The Jade Pot (*yuhu*) is where the transmutation occurs.

Lü Dongbin's *Baizi bei* (Hundred-Character Tablet) says:

氣回丹自結，壺中配坎離。

---

[10] *Jindan sibai zi*, in *Xiuzhen shishu*, chapter 5.

[11] *Ruyao jing*, in *Xiuzhen shishu*, chapter 13.

[12] Zi and Wu are symbolically represented by North and South, midnight and midday, or the winter and the summer solstices, respectively (note that in traditional Chinese cartography, the North is "below" and the South is "above"). Zi is the beginning of the Yang stage of a cycle, Wu is its culmination and the concurrent beginning of the Yin stage.

When Breath returns, the Elixir spontaneously coalesces:
within the pot, Kan and Li conjoin.

"Within the pot" refers to the place where the Elixir coalesces; in other words, it means the Tripod and the Stove. "Conjoin" means "transmute."

But although the alchemical texts employ a large number of images and metaphors, Zhang Boduan himself, in explaining the River Chariot, says that these principles of the practice should be applied with flexibility. In his *Four Hundred Words on the Golden Elixir*, he says:

震兌非東西，坎離不南北，斗柄運周天，要人會攢簇。

Zhen ☳ and Dui ☱ are not East and West,
Kan ☵ and Li ☲ are not South and North;
as the Dipper's handle revolves along the Celestial Circuit,
all people should gather together.[13]

In the postcelestial (*houtian*) arrangement of the eight trigrams, Zhen ☳ is at East, Dui ☱ at West, Li ☲ at South, and Kan ☵ at North (see table 4, top). In the precelestial (*xiantian*) arrangement, instead, Qian ☰ is at South, Kun ☷ at North, Li ☲ at East, and Kan ☵ at West (see table 4, bottom). Therefore the fire should be kindled at Kun to reach Qian; one should circulate the Fire of Li in the East in order to fill the Water of Kan in the West. The "handle" of the Northern Dipper represents the circulation along the Celestial Circuit. However, the third verse of the poem has an additional meaning: even though one knows the method of circulating of the River Chariot, during the refining one should apply flexibility, and should not adhere too rigidly to the literal meaning of the words.[14]

The verse, "all people should gather together" alludes to the "gathering together" of the five agents, which return to being "one family." In other words, during the circulation of the River Chariot, the Wood of Zhen ☳ and Xun ☴ joins the Fire of Li ☲ (the Original Spirit); the Metal of Qian ☰ and Dui ☱ joins the Water of Kan ☵ (the Original Essence); and Wood and Metal coalesce with the Soil of Kun ☷ and Gen ☶ (the True Intention, *zhenyi*). Then they are delivered to the Cinnabar Field, and they coagulate to form the Elixir.

Liu Qiaoqiao (1839–1933) wrote:

---

[13] *Jindan sibai zi*, poem 12.
[14] Wang Mu's remark apparently refers to the fact that the Dipper's handle does not literally "revolve along the Celestial Circuit."

下竅陰中有陽氣升，攝歸得中土即止。上竅陽中有陰氣降，得中
土即止。艮止之極，陽氣上蒸，木液下變，是為真汞；陰氣下
注，金精上升，變為真鉛。此乃真土之功。

In the lower Opening, the Yang Breath within the Yin rises; when it moves upwards and finds again the Central Soil, it pauses. In the upper Opening, the Yin Breath within the Yang descends; when it finds the Central Soil, it stops. After their pause culminates, the Yang Breath steams upward: the Liquor of Wood transforms itself below, and becomes True Mercury. The Yin Breath flows downward: the Essence of Metal rises above, and transforms itself into True Lead. This is the function of True Soil.[15]

The circulation of the Yin and Yang Breaths refers to the practice of the River Chariot. With regard to the circulation of the River Chariot, therefore, Zhang Boduan considers that since each person's circumstances are different, it should be applied with flexibility, and not by rigidly adhering to a model.

## The Fire Times (huohou 火候)

In the alchemical texts, Fire is a metaphor of Original Spirit. When Original Spirit coalesces with Essence and Breath, they circulate along the path of the Function and Control vessels. The operation of heating them as they begin to circulate is called Fire Times (huohou). The word "times" (hou, lit. "periods, spans of time") means "stages," and refers to the stages of advancement and withdrawal, slow and fast pace, and ascent and descent in the circulation of the External Medicine.

An alchemical text says:

進升主於採取，退降主於烹煉。其六陽時（子、醜、寅、卯、
辰、巳）火專於進升，六陰時（午、未、申、酉、戌、亥）火專
於下降。

[15] *Daoyuan jingwei ge*, "Xuanzhu chuanguan ge," section 4. Liu Qiaoqiao's passage is a note on the first poem in the *Jindan sibai si* (Four Hundred Words on the Golden Elixir): "True Soil seizes True Lead / True Lead controls True Mercury / Lead and Mercury return to True Soil / Body and mind are silent and unmoving."

Advancement and ascent rule on the collection [of the Medicine]; withdrawal and descent rule on the heating [of the Medicine]. In the six Yang times (those marked by Zi 子, Chou 丑, Yin 寅, Mao 卯, Chen 辰, and Si 巳), the Fire should advance and ascend. In the six Yin times (those marked by Wu 午, Wei 未, Shen 申, You 酉, Xu 戌, and Hai 亥), it should decrease and descend.[16]

The fast movement is called "fierce fire" (or "martial fire," *wuhuo*), and the slow one is called "gentle fire" (or "civil fire," *wenhuo*). To collect the Medicine, one always uses the "fierce fire." To heat and refine it, instead, one always uses the "gentle fire." An anonymous master said:

> 武火者，火逼金行也。文火者，舒徐而不迫促也。

> "Fierce fire" means that the Fire presses Metal into movement. "Gentle fire" means that it is calm and unhurried.

The *Zhenquan* (The Ultimate Truth) says:

> 火候本只寓一氣進退之節，非有他也。火候之妙在人，用意緊則火燥，用意緩則火寒。

> Fundamentally, the Fire Times consist only in the phases of advancement and withdrawal of the One Breath. The wonder of the Fire Times lies in oneself: if one's Intention is used too strongly, the Fire would scorch; if it is used too weakly, the Fire would chill.[17]

Therefore the term "fire times" in fact means nothing but the practice of cyclical refining.

In Taoism there is a saying: "The saints transmit the Medicine, but do not transmit the Fire; those who have known the Fire Times have always been few." The transmission of the Fire Times from master to disciple occurs only by means of oral instructions. Even *Awakening to Reality* is extremely cautious in its discussion of the Fire Times:

---

[16] These words appear to be paraphrased from a passage in Wu Shouyang's *Tianxian zhengli zhilun*, chapter 4. For the emblems mentioned in this passage, see table 8.

[17] *Zhenquan*, chapter 3, "Huohou." Wang Mu reproduces this passage from a slightly modified quotation found in Wu Shouyang's *Tianxian zhengli zhilun*, section 4, "Huohou jing."

契論經歌講至真，不將火候著於文，要知口訣通玄處，須共神仙
仔細論。

The *Token* and the treatises, the scriptures and the songs expound
　　ultimate Reality,
but do not commit the Fire Times to writing.
If you want to know the oral instructions and comprehend the
　　mysterious points,
you must discuss them in detail with a divine immortal.[18]

This means that the Fire Times cannot be put into writing, but at the
same time, they cannot be ignored. Another poem says:

縱識朱砂與黑鉛，不知火候也如閑，大都全借修持力，毫髮差殊
不結丹。

Even if you discern the Vermilion Cinnabar and the Black Lead,
it will be useless if you do not know the fire times.
On the whole, it all depends on the force of practice:
with the slightest error, the Elixir would not coalesce.[19]

In his commentary, Liu Yiming explains this poem as follows:

金丹全賴火候修持而成。火者修持之功力，候者修持之次序，採
藥須知遲早，煉藥須知時節。有文烹之火候，有武煉之火候，有
下手之火候，有止歇之火候，有進陽之火候，有退陰之火候，有
還丹之火候，有大丹之火候，有增減之火候，有溫養之火候，火
候居多，須要大澈大悟，知始知終，方能成功。

The formation of the Golden Elixir entirely depends on the practice
of the Fire Times. "Fire" means the force of the practice; "times"
means the sequence of the practice. When you collect the Medicine,
you must know what comes first and what comes after; when you
refine the Medicine, you must know the time segments. There are
the Fire Times of gentle ("civil") heating, and those of fierce ("martial") refining; those of the beginning, and those of the conclusion;
those of advancing the Yang, and those of withdrawing the Yin;
those of the Reverted Elixir (*huandan*), and those of the Great Elixir
(*dadan*); those of "augmenting and decreasing" (*zengjian*), and those
of "nourishing warmly" (*wenyang*). There are different types of Fire

---

[18] *Wuzhen pian*, "Jueju," poem 28. The *Token* is the *Zhouyi cantong qi*, or "Token
for the Joining of the Three in Accordance with the *Book of Changes*."
[19] *Wuzhen pian*, "Jueju," poem 27.

Times. You should comprehend them thoroughly, and know them from beginning to end. Only then can there be achievement.[20]

In his commentary to same poem of *Awakening to Reality*, Zhu Yuanyu writes:

真火者我之神，真候者我之息，以火煉藥而成丹，即是以神馭炁而證道也。

The true Fire is one's own Spirit; the true Times are one's own breathing. Refining the Medicine by means of Fire in order to form the Elixir is like Spirit driving Breath in order to attest to the Dao.[21]

Then Zhu Yuanyu breaks out of these conventional definitions, and adds, more comprehensively:

火候之秘，只在真意，大約念不可起，念起則火燥；意不可散，意散則火冷。只要一念不起，一意不散，時其動靜，察其寒溫，此修持行火之候也。

The secret of the Fire Times uniquely consists in the True Intention (*zhenyi*). Essentially, thoughts should not arise; if they arise, the Fire would scorch. The Intention should not disperse; if it disperses, the Fire would chill. No single thought should arise, and the single Intention should not disperse. One should time their movement and their quiescence, and control their cold and their heat. This is how one should practice the Fire Times.[22]

This passage provides a clear explanation of the principle of "advancing and withdrawing" in the Fire Times.

*The Cantong qi on the Fire Times.* Zhang Boduan's *Awakening to Reality* inherits and transmits the principles of the *Cantong qi*. The *Cantong qi* uses the hexagrams of the *Book of Changes* to explain the fire times of the Celestial Circuit:

朔旦為復，陽氣始通；… 臨爐施條，開路正光；… 仰以成泰，剛柔並隆；… 漸歷大壯，俠列卯門；… 夬陰以退，陽昇而前；

---

[20] *Wuzhen zhizhi*, "Jueju," commentary to poem 27.
[21] *Wuzhen pian chanyou*, "Jueju," commentary to poem 27.
[22] *Wuzhen pian chanyou*, id.

77

… 乾健盛明，廣被四鄰，陽終於巳，中而相干；… 姤始紀序，
履霜最先，井底寒泉，午為蕤賓；… 遯去世位，收斂其精；… 
否塞不通，萌者不生；… 觀其權量，察仲秋情；… 剝爛肢體，
消滅其形，化氣既竭，亡失至神，道窮則返，歸乎坤元。

The dawn of the first day of the month is Fu ䷖ (Return):
the Yang Breath begins to spread all through. . . .

At Lin ䷒ (Approach), the furnace issues strips of light,
opening the way for proper radiance. . . .

Looking upward, it forms Tai ䷊ (Peace):
the firm and the yielding both come to hold sway. . . .

Gradually comes the turn of Dazhuang ䷡ (Great Strength),
when the knights array themselves at the gates of Mao (卯). . . .

At Guai ䷪ (Parting) the time has come for Yin to move into retreat,
for Yang has risen and has come to the fore. . . .

Qian ䷀ (The Creative) is strong, flourishing, and bright,
and lays itself over the four neighborhoods.
Yang terminates at Si (巳);
residing in the Center, it has a share in everything. . . .

At Gou ䷫ (Encounter) a new epoch comes to pass:
for the first time there is hoarfrost underfoot.
In the well there is a clear, cold spring,
and at Luxuriant there is Wu (午). . . .

At Dun ䷠ (Withdrawal) it leaves its worldly place,
gathering its Essence to store it up. . . .

At Pi ䷋ (Obstruction) there are stagnation and blockade,
and no new buds are generated. . . .

Guan ䷓ (Contemplation), with its equity and its balance,
examines the temper of autumn's middle month. . . .

Bo ䷖ (Splitting Apart) tears its limbs and trunk,
extinguishing its form.
The vital Breath is drained,
the supreme Spirit is forgotten and is lost. . . .

> The course comes to its end and turns around,
> returning to its origin in Kun ☷ (The Receptive)....[23]

This poem describes transmutation in six Yang and six Yin stages, called "ebb and flow" (*xiaoxi*, see table 6). The Yang is firm and the Yin is yielding; when the firm culminates, it transforms itself into the yielding.

According to the alchemical texts, the main requirement at the stage of "refining Essence and transmuting it into Breath" is that the Yang Essence be refined and transmuted. The hexagram Fu ䷗, formed by Earth ☷ and Thunder ☳, is called "the birth of initial Yang" (*yiyang sheng*). This Yang should be collected and refined by going through the six Yang stages until it reaches the pure Qian ☰. The firm Yang grows until it culminates, and when something culminates, it is followed by an inversion. This is a metaphor to indicate that although the Yang Essence is already abundant, it is still a material entity and thus cannot form the Medicine; it should first be turned from firm to yielding, and then be transmuted. Therefore, as the Essence goes through the six Yin stages, it is progressively transmuted until it exhausts its firm, material Breath, and forms a "Breath" [炁] made of the union of Essence and Breath. In this way, one reaches the goal of "joining the Three into the Two."

The *Daode jing* says:

> 載營魄抱一，能無離乎？專氣致柔，能嬰兒乎？

> In carrying and maintaining your *po*-soul and in embracing Unity,
> can you not separate from them?
> In concentrating your breath until it is at its softest,
> can you be like an infant?[24]

"Advancing the Yang Fire" in order to exhaust the firm breath (*gangqi*), and "withdrawing by the Yin response" in order to attain the soft breath (*rouqi*), are the practice of "concentrating breath until it is at its softest." When one performs the Lesser Celestial Circuit, the upward stage is called "advancing the Yang Fire" (*jin yanghuo*), and "Fire pressing Metal into movement" (*huo bi jinxing*). After Breath reaches the Muddy Pellet, one "withdraws by the Yin response" (*tui yinfu*), and the firm breath is transmuted by means of the True Yang Breath. In his commentary to the *Cantong qi*, Liu Yiming says: "'Withdrawing by the Yin response' means

---

[23] *Cantong qi*, chapter 19.
[24] *Daode jing*, 10.

that Yin and Yang tally with one another. In other words, when Yang culminates, it should be nourished by means of the Yin."[25]

*Zhang Boduan on the Fire Times.* In his *Awakening to Reality*, Zhang Boduan elaborates on the discourse of the *Cantong qi*. One of its poems says:

虎躍龍騰風浪麤，中央正位產玄珠，果生枝上終期熟，子在胞中豈有殊。南北宗源翻卦象，晨昏火候合天樞，須知大隱居廛市，何必深山守靜孤。

The Tiger leaps, the Dragon soars,
wind and waves are rough;
in the correct position of the center
the Mysterious Pearl is born.
A fruit grows on the branches
and ripens at the end of season:
could the Child in the womb
be different from this?

Between South and North, the ancestral source
causes the hexagrams to revolve;
from daybreak to dusk, the fire times
accord with the Celestial Axis.
You should know the great concealment
while you dwell in the market place:
what need is there of entering the mountains' depths
and keeping yourself in stillness and solitude?[26]

"Wind and waves" refers to the circulation of Essence and Breath. "The correct position of the center" refers to the Cinnabar Field (or, according to another interpretation, to the Yellow Court), and "Mysterious Pearl" is another name of the Internal Elixir. "The ancestral source between South and North" corresponds to the verses quoted below from the *Cantong qi*,

---

[25] *Cantong zhizhi,* "Jingwen," chapter 1. Here Wang Mu summarizes Liu Yiming's words: "'Yin response' (*yinfu*) means that when Yang culminates, it should be nourished by means of the Yin. When the Yin nourishes the Yang, the Yang Breath is not overbearing; this means that Yin and Yang tally with one another. The Yin in the expression 'Yin response' is not the Yin of the extraneous breaths (*keqi*) that come from the outside, but the True Yin collected from the True Yang. On the one hand, the True Yang retreats; on the other, the True Yin grows."

[26] *Wuzhen pian,* "Lüshi," poem 5.

"Zi at South, Wu at North, are each other's guiding thread" (see below, p. 102). Zi 子 means the Meeting of Yin cavity, from which the six Yang stages begin their ascent, and Wu 午 means the Palace of the Muddy Pellet (*niwan gong*), from which the six Yin stages begin their descent. Both are positions within the human body. The *Cantong qi* also says:

天符有進退 … 昇降據斗樞。

The tallies of Heaven advance and withdraw . . .
rise and fall depend on the axis of the Dipper.[27]

Zhang Boduan similarly writes that "the fire times accord with the Celestial Axis." In this verse, Celestial Axis (*tianshu*) is the name of the first star of the Northern Dipper: the circulation of the River Chariot is modeled on the rotation of the Dipper in heaven. "The hexagrams revolve" refers to the turning upside down of the six Yin and the six Yang hexagrams, which in turn represent the twelve stages of the Fire Times. Since the hexagrams follow a cyclical sequence (see table 6), they are said to "revolve." Zi 子 and Wu 午 are together the "ancestral source," i.e., the central point; they allow the ascent and the descent, the opening and the closing in the practice of the Celestial Circuit.

When Zhang Boduan's poem quoted above says that the Fire Times revolve "from daybreak to dusk," this is a metaphor alluding to the increase and decrease of Fire. In another poem, Zhang Boduan explains the meaning of "daybreak and dusk" as follows:

天地才交否泰，朝昏好識屯蒙，輻來輳轂水朝宗，妙在抽添運用。

Heaven and Earth at last conjoin through Pi ䷋ and Tai ䷊,
morning and dusk know one another through Zhun ䷂ and Meng ䷃.
The spokes converge onto the hub, Water returns to the source:
the wonder lies in the operation of lessening and augmenting.[28]

The Zhun ䷂ hexagram is made of the trigrams for Water ☵ and Thunder ☳, and represents the ascending Sun in the morning: the initial Yang, carrying Water, ascends from the Caudal Funnel (Water is an emblem of the ingredient of the Elixir). The Meng ䷃ hexagram is made of the trigrams for Mountain ☶ and Water ☵, and represents the Sun after

[27] *Cantong qi*, chapter 4.
[28] *Wuzhen pian*, "Xijiang yue," poem 8.

noon: the initial Yang, following Water, descends from the Muddy Pellet. According to another explanation, the first line of the Zhun hexagram is the "initial Yang," and is an image of the rising Yang; the first line of the Meng hexagram is a Yin line, and is an image of the declining Yin. An alchemical text says:

水雷屯系震卦為主，地下雷轟火逼金之象也。山水蒙系艮卦為主，陽剛已止轉為陰柔，專氣致柔，精化為炁之象也。

Zhun ䷂, which is made of Water ☵ and Thunder ☳, is ruled by the trigram Zhen ☳. Under the earth there is a crack of thunder: this is an image of Fire pressing onto Metal.

Meng ䷃, which is made of Mountain ☶ and Water ☵, is ruled by the trigram Gen ☶. The firmness of Yang has ceased, and has changed into the yieldingness of Yin: this is an image of Breath becoming extremely soft, and of Essence transmuting itself into Breath.[29]

This is equivalent to saying that the alchemical practice should correspond to the hexagrams of the "twelve-stage ebb and flow" (shi'er xiaoxi), i.e., to the cyclical path of the River Chariot. Therefore the poem of *Awakening to Reality* quoted above says that Heaven and Earth "at last conjoin." This is also what Shao Yong mentions in his "Chant of the Vague and Indistinct":

恍惚陰陽初變化，氤氳天地乍回旋。

Vague and indistinct, Yin and Yang begin to transform;
misty and murky, Heaven and Earth for the first time revolve.[30]

Let us return to the poem of *Awakening to Reality* quoted above. In the hexagrams Pi ䷋ and Tai ䷊, the positions of the Yin (☷) and Yang (☰) halves are respectively inverted; and as for the transformation from Zhun ䷂ to Meng ䷃, both hexagrams are based on Water,[31] and therefore indicate the transmutation of the Medicine. Thus the poem of *Awakening to Reality* says that morning and dusk "know one another." Zhang Boduan tells his readers that they should know these principles when they refine

---

[29] Wang Mu attributes this passage to Liu Yiming, but it is not found in any of Liu Yiming's works. I have not been able to identify its source.

[30] Shao Yong, *Huanghu jin*.

[31] The Zhun ䷂ hexagram is made of the trigrams for Water ☵ and Thunder ☳, and the Meng ䷃ hexagram is made of the trigrams for Mountain ☶ and Water ☵.

the Medicine by means of the Lesser Celestial Circuit, so that they can refine Essence into Breath and complete the "initial barrier" of the refining of the Elixir. That the images of the hexagrams Zhun and Meng are reciprocally inverted is also alluded to by the metaphor that "the hexagrams revolve," found in another poem of *Awakening to Reality* quoted above.

As we have seen (p. 57), a poem by Shao Yong says:

乾遇巽時觀月窟，地逢雷處見天根，天根月窟閑來往，三十六宮
皆是春。

When Qian (Heaven ☰) meets Xun (Wind ☴), contemplate the
    Moon's Lair,
when the Earth (Kun ☷) comes across the Thunder (Zhen ☳),
    observe the Heaven's Root.
Leisurely go back and forth between the Moon's Lair and the
    Heaven's Root:
in all the thirty-six palaces it is spring.[32]

The Cavity of the Moon's Lair (*yueku xue*) is in the Muddy Pellet (or according to some, in the point between the two eyebrows), and the Heaven's Root (*tiangen*) is the Meeting of Yin cavity. They respectively correspond to the hexagrams Zhun ䷂ (the place where the fire is kindled) and Meng ䷃ (the place where the decrease of Fire begins). Water is a code name of Original Essence.

*The three chariots.* When the alchemical practice reaches the time of collecting the Medicine, the Fire Times go through three stages, called the "sheep chariot" (*yangche*), the "deer chariot" (*luche*), and the "ox chariot" (*niuche*). From the Barrier of the Caudal Funnel to the Barrier of the Spinal Handle, one should proceed carefully and with a short pace, similar to the lightness of a chariot drawn by a sheep. From the Barrier of the Spinal Handle to the Barrier of the Jade Pillow, one should proceed quickly and in large steps, similar to the nimbleness of a chariot drawn by a deer. From the Barrier of the Jade Pillow to the Muddy Pellet, since the Barrier of the Jade Pillow is extremely fine and subtle, one should charge forward with much power, similar to the strength of a chariot drawn by an ox. These similitudes apply to the stage in which the Medicine has been formed. They are referred to in the saying, "Loading gold on three

---

[32] Shao Yong, *Guanwu jin* (Chant on the Contemplation of Things).

83

chariots, you ascend to Mount Kunlun," and they are also the meaning of the verse, "The spokes converge onto the hub, Water returns to the source" quoted above from a poem of *Awakening to Reality*.[33]

*Images and metaphors.* The expression "bathing at Mao (卯) and You (酉)" (*maoyou muyu*), used in the Fire Times, is borrowed from the divinatory arts. In Neidan, it means that when the circulation of Breath reaches those points, it should briefly pause. Although this corresponds to the positions of Mao and You, i.e., the navel in the front and the kidneys in the back, the expression "bathing at Mao and You" actually refers to the shift that occurs when, during the circulation of the River Chariot, the ascending stage turns into the descending stage, and the descending stage turns into the ascending stage. This is why Zhang Boduan says in his *Four Hundred Words on the Golden Elixir*:

火候不用時，冬至不在子，及其沐浴法，卯酉時虛比。

The Fire Times have no times,
the winter solstice is not at Zi (子);
and as for the method of bathing,
the times of Mao and You are empty similitudes.[34]

These words tell us that trigrams and hexagrams are only metaphors; they should not be seen with a rigid attitude, and everyone should awaken to them by oneself.

This is not only true of "bathing": with regard to the "twelve-stage ebb and flow" (*shi'er xiaoxi*), and to the ascent and descent according to Zhun ䷂ and Meng ䷃, Zhang Boduan again tells us that they all require flexibility. Moreover, as we have already seen, another poem in the *Four Hundred Words* says:

震兌非東西，坎離不南北，斗柄運周天，要人會攢簇。

Zhen ☳ and Dui ☱ are not East and West,
Kan ☵ and Li ☲ are not South and North;
as the Dipper's handle revolves along the Celestial Circuit,
all people should gather together.[35]

---

[33] *Wuzhen pian*, "Xijiang yue," poem 8.
[34] *Jindan sibai zi*, poem 13.
[35] *Jindan sibai zi*, poem 12.

Here Zhang Boduan points out that the alchemical practice should be flexible and not rigid, and that the lines of the trigrams and the hexagrams do not have an absolute value. *Awakening to Reality* also says:

卦中設象本儀形，得象忘言意自明，舉世迷徒惟執象，卻行卦氣望飛昇。

> The images of the hexagrams are established on the basis of their
>     meanings:
> understand the images and forget the words — the idea is clear of
>     itself.
> The whole world delusively clings to the images:
> they practice the "breaths of the hexagrams" and hope thereby to
>     rise in flight.[36]

Liu Yiming's commentary to this poem says that trigrams and hexagrams are nothing more than forms and images used to clarify the principles of Yin and Yang; however, the deluded disciples of our time do not understand their meaning. For example, he continues, the sixty-four hexagrams begin with Zhun ䷂ and Meng ䷃, and end with Jiji ䷾ and Weiji ䷿.[37] Therefore those disciples practice in conformity to Zhun in the morning, and in conformity to Meng in the evening. This is a great error. They do not know, says Liu Yiming, that "the birth of Yang is Zhun, and the fall of Yang is Meng. The birth of Yang is like the morning at daytime, and the fall of Yang is like the evening at nighttime. When Yang is born, advancing the Yang Fire (*jin yanghuo*) in order to collect the Yang is called 'Zhun in the morning.' When Yang falls, cycling the Yin response in order to nourish the Yang is called 'Meng in the evening.'" As for Jiji and Weiji, they only mean the coagulation of Yin and Yang with one another.[38]

---

[36] *Wuzhen pian*, "Jueju," poem 37. "Rising in flight" is an allusion to becoming immortal.

[37] Liu Yiming refers to the cycle of sixty hexagrams during the thirty days of the lunar month. In this cycle, Qian ䷀, Kun ䷁, Kan ䷜, and Li ䷝ are omitted. The remaining hexagrams are associated in pairs with the first and the second halves of each day (see table 5). Therefore, in the first day of the month, Zhun ䷂ rules in the morning and Meng ䷃ rules in the evening, and so forth for the remaining days.

[38] This paragraph is partly quoted, partly paraphrased from Liu Yiming's *Wuzhen zhizhi*, "Jueju," commentary to poem 37.

To conclude, one should not become mired in the alchemical images. Fire should be applied in a natural way;[39] only then is it possible to respond to the requirements of the alchemical practice.

## *Tripod and Stove* (dinglu 鼎爐)

The terms "tripod" and "stove" derive from External Alchemy. They represent the places in which the Golden Elixir is refined. The tripod is in the Palace of the Muddy Pellet (i.e., the upper Cinnabar Field), and the stove is in the lower Cinnabar Field. In the circulation of the River Chariot, the External Medicine rises to the Muddy Pellet, then descends and coagulates in the "earthenware crucible" (*tufu*); in other words, it rises along the Control vessel and reaches the top of the head, then descends from the top of the head along the Function vessel and enters the lower Cinnabar Field. This stage of the alchemical practice is called the "Great Tripod and Stove" (*da dinglu*).

*Awakening to Reality* says:

> 先把乾坤為鼎器，次搏烏兔藥來烹，既驅二物歸黃道，爭得金丹不解生。

> First take Qian and Kun as the tripod and the stove,
> then catch the crow and the hare and boil the Medicine.
> Once you have chased the two things and they have returned to the
>     Yellow Path,
> how could the Golden Elixir not be born?[40]

This poem enunciates the positions of the tripod and the stove. Qian ☰ is Heaven and is above, Kun ☷ is the Earth and is below. The crow in the Sun and the hare in the Moon are Kan ☵ and Li ☲, respectively. The Sun represents Original Spirit, and the Moon represents Original Essence. When they are collected, they are led onto the Yellow Path (*huangdao*), which is another name of the River Chariot. Making them pause when they reach the top of the head is called "eliminating the ore in order to

---

[39] The expression used by Wang Mu, *ziru*, is a synonym of *ziran*, "spontaneous, natural, so of its own."

[40] *Wuzhen pian*, "Jueju," poem 1.

keep the gold" (*qukuang liujin*); making them descend from the top of the head is called "delivering the Medicine to the stove" (*suanyao guilu*). These are the functions of the Tripod and Stove with regard to the refining of Essence, Breath, and Spirit. In practice, they represent the cyclical process required for compounding the Medicine.

The *Dinglu shi* (Poem on the Tripod and the Stove) by Qingxia zi says:

> 鼎鼎非金鼎，爐爐非玉爐，火從臍下發，水向頂中符。三姓自會合，二物自相拘，固濟胎不泄，變化在須臾。

> The tripod, the tripod — is not the golden tripod,
> the stove, the stove — is not the jade stove.
> Fire issues from the navel and goes downward,
> Water from the summit responds to it.
> The three families meet and join,
> the two things seize one another.
> Firmly seal the embryo, so that there are no leaks,
> and the transformation will happen in one instant.[41]

By means of Fire, the Original Spirit moves upward, and with the aid of Water, the Original Essence enters the tripod. The "three families" are also mentioned in *Awakening to Reality*:

> 自稱木液與金精，遇土卻成三姓。

> They call themselves Liquor of Wood and Essence of Metal,
> and when they meet Soil, they form the three families.[42]

This means that Original Essence and Original Spirit, the "two families," coagulate by means of the Intention-Soil (*yitu*). When the "two fives" wondrously join with one another, they are called the "three families." In fact, this refers to the "gathering together" (*cuancu*) of the five agents.[43] *Awakening to Reality* says:

---

[41] Quoted in *Xingming guizhi*, "Yuan ji."

[42] *Wuzhen pian*, "Xijiang yue," poem 5.

[43] These very concise statements essentially mean that, according to the "generation numbers" of the five agents, Water (1) and Metal (4) amount to 5; Fire (2) and Wood (3) also amount to 5; and Soil by itself has a value of 5. When the first and second pairs of agents join to one another, there are "three families," each of which has a numerical value of 5. Then the Water-Metal and the Fire-Wood pairs of agents merge through the intermediation of Soil, and the five agents are "gathered together" to their original state of unity.

二物會時情性合，五行全處龍虎蟠。

When the two things meet,
emotions and nature join one another;
where the five agents are whole,
Dragon and Tiger coil.[44]

The "two things" are Yin and Yang; when they are conjoined, they form the Numinous Medicine (*lingyao*). "Sealing firmly" means that after Water and Fire have been equalized, one should tightly close the "chamber of the seed" (*zhongshi*) without allowing any leaks. All this reflects the verses of the *Cantong qi* that say:

先液而後凝，號曰黃輿焉。

First it liquefies, then coagulates;
it is given the name Yellow Carriage.[45]

This is the function of the Great Tripod and Stove.

At the stage of "refining Breath to transmute it into Spirit," the Great Tripod and Stove are not used, and one uses instead the Small Tripod and Stove (*xiao dinglu*). Above, the Yellow Court is the tripod, and below, the Cinnabar Field is the stove. The space of murky and misty Breath within the two cavities is guarded in quiescence by means of Spirit, and no cycling occurs along the Function and Control vessels. Therefore the Great Tripod and Stove pertain to the initial stage, and the Small Tripod and Stove pertain to the intermediate stage of the practice.

### "Collecting," "Sealing," "Refining," and "Extinguishing" (cai 採, feng 封, lian 煉, zhi 止)

The terms "collecting," "sealing," "refining," and "extinguishing" describe the completion of the process of "refining Essence and transmuting it into Breath." Together, they are called "the four oral instructions" (*si koujue*).

---

[44] *Wuzhen pian*, "Lüshi," poem 3.
[45] *Cantong qi*, chapter 14.

*Awakening to Reality* says about the collection of the Medicine:

要知產藥川源處，只在西南是本鄉，鉛遇癸生須急採，金逢望遠
不堪嘗。

> You should know that the source of the stream,
> the place where the Medicine is born,
> is just at the southwest —
> that is its native village.
> When Lead meets the birth of *gui*,
> quickly you should collect it:
> if Metal goes past the full moon,
> it is not fit to be savored.[46]

This poem says that the "mother of the Elixir" (*danmu*), made of Essence, Breath, and Spirit, is born in the "southwest," i.e., the abdomen. After the Medicine is born, it should be collected and moved to the "stove." Since the birth of the Medicine occurs at a definite time—the so-called "living Zi hour" (*huo zishi*)—there should not be errors.[47]

The same poem continues by saying:

送歸土釜牢封閉，次入流珠廝配當，藥重一斤須二八，調停火候
託陰陽。

> Send it back to the earthenware crucible,
> seal it tightly,
> then add the Flowing Pearl,
> so that they are match for one another.
> For the Medicine to weigh one pound
> the Two Eights are needed;
> regulate the fire times
> relying on Yin and Yang.[48]

The second half of the poem mentions "sealing tightly" (*lao fengbi*), a synonym of "sealing firmly" seen in the previous section. The "earthenware crucible" is the Cinnabar Field (whose location is not the same as the one mentioned in the medical texts). "Then add the Flowing Pearl, so that they are match for one another" means that Original Spirit and Original Essence join one another. Concerning the verse "For the

---

[46] *Wuzhen pian,* "Lüshi," poem 7.
[47] On the "living Zi hour" see below, pp. 106 ff.
[48] *Wuzhen pian,* id.

Medicine to weigh one pound the Two Eights are needed," it should be remembered that in the ancient Chinese weight system, one pound (*jin*) is equivalent to sixteen ounces (*liang*). Therefore "two eights" means half a pound of Metal and half a pound of Water: the metaphor is both material and immaterial. The final verse, "Regulate the fire times relying on Yin and Yang," concerns the refining of the Medicine. By means of the circulation of the River Chariot, one first "advances the Fire" and then "responds by withdrawing"; thus the firm Yang is changed into the yielding Yin. It is sent again to the stove in the Cinnabar Field, where "the ore is eliminated and gold is pure." This generates an immaterial Breath, which is the "mother of the Elixir" (*danmu*).

The so-called "collection," "sealing," and "refining" constitute a series of methods of "doing" (*youwei*), and this is a point of crucial importance in "refining Essence and transmuting it into Breath." After the "sealing," the newly-obtained Medicine is again refined, and at the end of three hundred cycles of refining it forms the Great Medicine (*dayao*). *Awakening to Reality* refers to this when it says:

真精既返黃金室，一顆靈光永不離。

Once True Essence has returned to the chamber of Yellow Gold,
The one pearl of Numinous Radiance will never part.[49]

This is what the *Daode jing* calls "returning to the root and reverting to life" (*fangen fuming*).[50] Another poem in *Awakening to Reality* says:

萬物芸芸各返根，返根復命即常存。

The ten thousand things, in all their multiplicity, return to the root;
as they return to the root and revert to life, they are constantly
    preserved.[51]

This poem provides further details on this subject.

After "collection," "sealing," and "refining" have gone through the three hundred cycles of refining, a Yang radiance (*yangguang*) appears before one's eyes. When it appears twice, the Fire must be extinguished. Another poem says:

---

[49] *Wuzhen pian*, "Jueju," poem 39.
[50] *Daode jing*, 16.
[51] *Wuzhen pian*, "Jueju," poem 51.

未煉還丹須急煉，煉了還須知止足，若還持盈未已心，不免一朝遭殆辱。

If you have not yet refined the Reverted Elixir, then quickly refine it; having refined it, you should know how to stop when it is enough. If you still hold it and fill your mind with it, instead of halting it, you will not avoid danger, and before long will suffer humiliation.[52]

This poem refers to the point in which the efficacy of one's practice has reached achievement, and the breath (*qi*) of the Medicine is abundant. "Doing" has bloomed, and "non-doing" becomes manifest. Liu Yiming's commentary on this poem says:

還者，還其所本有，如物已失而復得，已去而仍還也。若丹已還，當速住火停輪，用溫養之功。

"Reverting" means returning to what is fundamentally already there. It is as though something has been lost and is recovered, or someone has left and returns. When the Elixir has reverted, immediately extinguish the Fire and halt its revolving. [Then] use the operation of "nourishing warmly" (*wenyang*).[53]

At that time, one can enter the stage of "refining Breath to transmute it into Spirit." Since Essence and Breath have coalesced with one another, "the Three have returned to the Two." Essence has been transmuted and is exhausted, and has become True Breath (*zhenqi*). The next step consists in refining this Breath and transmuting it into Spirit: this is the process by which "the Two return to the One."

## Conclusion

What we have described in this chapter is the first step of the practice according to the alchemical texts. After the Southern and the Northern Lineages of Neidan were merged by Chen Zhixu (1290–ca. 1368) in the late

---

[52] *Wuzhen pian*, "Jueju," poem 61. The third verse alludes to the first sentence of *Daode jing*, 9: "You hold something to fill it up, but this is not as good as halting."

[53] Quoted, with some omissions, from Liu Yiming's *Wuzhen zhizhi*, "Jueju," commentary to poem 61.

Yuan period, the respective alchemical practices gradually converged. Instead of the division into Northern and Southern lineages, the emphasis shifted to the methods of self-cultivation themselves. With the exception of the Yin-Yang branch (Yinyang pai), which maintained its own line of transmission, the Pure Cultivation branch (Qingxiu pai) was not divided into Northern and Southern branches. During the Ming dynasty, not only it integrated and blended the Northern and Southern practices, but it also absorbed certain principles of Chan Buddhism, and partly assimilated the Confucian methods of self-cultivation. This convergence resulted into the alchemical practices of "the Three Teachings joined into one."

In this and the previous chapters, we have described the processes for "laying the foundations" and for "refining Essence and transmuting it into Breath." These processes constitute together the first part of the alchemical practice. They consist of practical methods, which Taoism deems to be the gateways to self-cultivation. Even though they are not entirely devoid of idealistic components, there is evidence that they can cure illnesses and preserve health.

In the two early alchemical scriptures, the *Cantong qi* and the *Ruyao jing*, the four stages of the alchemical practice are not yet clearly set forth. In the *Zhong-Lü chuandao ji* (Records of the Transmission of the Dao from Zhongli Quan to Lü Dongbin) and the *Xishan qunxian huizhen ji* (Records of the Immortals and the True Men of the Western Mountain), both written by Shi Jianwu (Tang dynasty), the three main stages are called "refining the form to transmute it into Breath" (*lianxing huaqi*), "refining Breath to transmute it into Spirit" (*lianqi huashen*), and "refining Spirit to join with the Dao" (*lianshen hedao*). A gloss states that "refining the form" (*lianxing*) is equivalent to "refining the Essence" (*lianjing*). The *Xishan qunxian huizhen ji* also refers to a fourth stage, "refining the Dao to achieve sainthood" (*liandao chengsheng*), which is not mentioned in other texts. It should be noted that there were two persons named Shi Jianwu; one was a poet who lived during the Tang dynasty (618–907), the other was a Taoist master who lived during the Song dynasty (960–1279). However, since all Taoist texts state that Shi Jianwu lived during the Tang dynasty, I deem his works to be representative of the Tang period.

During the Five Dynasties (907–60), Chen Tuan (ca. 920–89) engraved the *Wuji tu* (Chart of the Ultimateless) on the walls of a cavern on Mount Hua (Huashan, in present-day Shaanxi). Zhu Yizun's (1629–1709) *Taiji tu shoushou kao* (Study of the Transmission of the *Chart of the Ultimate*) says:

圖形自下而上：初一曰玄牝之門（丹經解為指示丹法始基的玄關
一竅）；次二曰煉精化炁，煉氣化神；次三曰五行定位，五氣朝
元（丹經解為鉛汞的運用）；再次曰陰陽配合，取坎填離；最上
曰煉神還虛，復歸無極。

From bottom to top, the Chart depicts:

1 The Gate of the Mysterious-Female (*xuanpin zhi men*, explained by
   the alchemical texts to be the One Opening of the Mysterious
   Barrier at the beginning of the practice)
2 "Refining Essence and transmuting it into Breath"
3 The positions of the five agents, and the "return of the five
   agents to the source" (*wuqi chaoyuan*, explained by the alchemical
   texts to be the operation of Lead and Mercury)
4 The conjunction of Yin and Yang, or "taking from Kan ☵ in order
   to fill Li ☲"
5 On top, "refining Spirit to return to Emptiness," or "returning to
   the Ultimateless"

Although the *Chart* is made of five sections, they correspond to the three
main stages of the alchemical practice. Zhang Boduan and Chen Tuan
were contemporaries, and both adhered to the alchemical methods of Lü
Dongbin; therefore there are no discrepancies in the respective alchemical teachings. Although Zhang Boduan does not clearly describe the
stages of the practice in his *Awakening to Reality*, in the preface to his *Four
Hundred Words on the Golden Elixir* he explicitly states that one transforms
Essence into Breath, Breath into Spirit, and Spirit into Emptiness. He calls
this process "the three flowers gather at the sinciput" (*sanhua juding*).
Essentially, in his view, the two homophone words *hua* 花 ("flower") and
*hua* 化 ("transformation") both refer to "refining."[54]

The Pure Cultivation branch (Qingxiu pai) of the Southern Lineage
inherited and continued to transmit these methods of self-cultivation.
Chen Niwan (?–1213) transmitted them to Bai Yuchan (1194–1229?), who
elaborated them further. In his *Kuaihuo ge* (Song of Joyful Life), Bai
Yuchan says:

忘形養氣乃金液，對景無心是大還，忘形化氣氣化神，斯乃大道
透三關。

Forget the forms and nourish Breath — this is the Golden Liquor;
look onto the scene in front of you with no-mind — this is the Great
Return.

[54] *Jindan sibai zi*, in *Xiuzhen shishu*, chapter 5, preface.

Forget the forms and transmute Breath, then transmute Breath into
Spirit —
this is the Great Dao passing through the three barriers.[55]

During the Yuan dynasty, Li Daochun (fl. ca. 1290), a second-generation disciple of Bai Yuchan and a direct disciple of Wang Jinchan, wrote
his *Zhonghe ji* (Collection of Central Harmony). Li Daochun was well-
versed in the principles of the Three Teachings—Confucianism,
Buddhism, and Taoism—and integrated the Pure Cultivation alchemical
methods of the Southern and the Northern lineages of Quanzhen with
one another. In the *Zhonghe ji*, he clearly refers to the three stages, saying:

煉精化氣，煉氣化神，煉神還虛，謂之三花聚鼎，又謂之三關。

Refining Essence to transmute it into Breath, refining Breath to
transmute it into Spirit, refining Spirit to return to Emptiness: this
is called "the three flowers gather in the tripod." (The "tripod" is
equivalent to the sinciput.) It is also called the "three barriers."[56]

In one of the poems found in the same work, Li Daochun says:

三元大藥意心身，著意心身便系塵，調息要調真息息，煉神須煉
不神神。頓忘物我三花聚，猛棄機緣五氣臻，八達四通無窒礙，
隨時隨處闡全真。

The Great Medicines of the Three Origins are intention, mind, and
body,
but if you are attached to intention, mind, and body, they are like
the dust of this world.
To harmonize breathing, you should harmonize the breathing of
true breathing;
to refine Spirit, you must refine the Spirit that is not Spirit.
As you immediately forget self and other, the Three Flowers gather
together;
as you powerfully discard motives and conditions, the Five Breaths
arrive.
On the eight roads and the four thoroughfares there are no obstructions:
at all times and in all places, you disclose the Complete Reality.[57]

---

[55] *Xiuzhen shishu*, chapter 39.
[56] *Zhonghe ji*, chapter 3. The sentence in parentheses is added by Wang Mu.
[57] *Zhonghe ji*, chapter 5, "Shu gongfu."

This poem contains the essence of the three stages of alchemical cultivation.

The authors and texts cited above are associated with the transmission of the Pure Cultivation branch (Qingxiu pai) of Neidan. The views of the Yin-Yang branch (Yinyang pai) are different. Chen Zhixu, who merged the Southern and Northern lineages of Quanzhen, was an exponent of the Yin-Yang branch, but also gave importance to the Pure Cultivation branch. In his *Jindan dayao* (Great Essentials of the Golden Elixir), he often explains the Pure Cultivation. As we saw at the beginning of this book, he accounts for the reason of the subdivision into stages saying:

> 萬物含三，三歸二，二歸一。知此道者，怡神守形，養形鍊精，積精化氣，鍊氣合神，鍊神還虛，金丹乃成。

> The ten thousand things hold the Three, the Three return to the Two, the Two return to the One. Those who know this Way look after their Spirit and guard their corporeal form. They nourish the corporeal form to refine the Essence, accumulate the Essence to transmute it into Breath, refine the Breath to merge it with Spirit, and refine the Spirit to revert to Emptiness. Then the Golden Elixir is achieved.[58]

Chen Zhixu's discourse was made possible by the fact that, after the merging of the Southern and Northern lineages of Quanzhen in the late Yuan period, the Pure Cultivation branch was free of the boundaries of "southern" and "northern," and only stood in opposition to the Yin-Yang branch.

In the late Ming period, the eighth-generation master of Quanzhen, Wu Shouyang (1574–1644), assembled the achievements of the earlier masters of the Pure Cultivation branch. His works include the *Tianxian zhengli zhilun* (Straightforward Discourses on the Correct Principles of Celestial Immortality), the *Dandao jiupian* (Nine Essays on the Way of the Elixir), and the *Xian Fo hezong yulu* (Recorded Sayings on the Common Origin of the Immortals and the Buddhas). In these works, Wu Shouyang provides a complete and detailed exposition of the three stages of the alchemical practice and the respective methods. In the *Dandao jiupian*, he calls "laying the foundations" the "earliest return to Emptiness" (*zuichu huanxu*) and the "earliest practice of self-refining" (*zuichu lianji gongfu*).

---

[58] *Jindan dayao*, chapter 4.

By his time, the systematization of the alchemical practice into four stages had already been accomplished.

In the present book, emphasis has been given to explicating the terminology pertaining to the first two steps of the practice. This is because, after the bodily functions have been restored through the practices of "laying the foundations," the goal of "refining Essence and transmuting it into Breath" is the further extension of bodily strength, and the further flourishing of the life force (*shengming li*). Decay turns into vigor, and what was not there becomes apparent. This is the function of "transmutation" (*hua*).

"The three transmutations are the three transformations of the three stages of refining." This saying might appear to possess a mystical nature, but actually only means harmonizing blood and breath, cultivating one's mind, balancing one's nervous system, actualizing one's youthful vigor, controlling the body by means of the mind, and using an inner method that allows the bodily functions to receive what is proper to them, in order to reach the goal of healing illnesses and extending the length of life. It is not an otherworldly saying.

The alchemical masters of the past had to observe interdictions, and concealed what is easy under difficult and profound words. They employed many metaphoric terms, using lines, tigrams, and hexagrams of the *Yijing* (Book of Changes); the celestial stems (*tiangan*) and the earthly branches (*dizhi*), for example in the system of Matching the Stems (*najia*); Water, Fire, and the other agents; and alchemical emblems such as gold, lead, cinnabar, and mercury.[59] These masters hided the head and displayed the tail, discussed the mystery but spoke of the wondrous. For this reason, researchers have troubles in finding clues, and practitioners boast their supernatural powers. However, this stage of the practice is nothing but a particular type of Taoist Qigong. It is plain and easy, and does not claim transmission from gods or immortals, or any "numinous mechanism" or "wondrous art." It just tells practitioners to arduously practice in order to reinforce their convictions.

During the Yuan dynasty, Li Daochun wrote in his *Zhonghe ji*:

---

[59] "Matching the Stems" is a representation of the cycle of the Moon by means of cosmological emblems. Each of the six five-day periods of the month is associated with one of the eight trigrams (Zhen ☳, Dui ☱, Qian ☰, Xun ☴, Gen ☶, and Kun ☷, respectively). Each trigram, moreover, is associated with one of the ten celestial stems (Geng 庚, Ding 丁, Jia 甲, Xin 辛, Bing 丙, and Yi 乙). This pattern, originally created by the Han-dynasty cosmologists, became one of the models for the practice of the "fire times" (*huohou*) in Internal Alchemy.

予前所言，金丹之大概，若向這裏具只眼，方信大事不在紙上。
其或未然，須知下手處，既知下手處，便從下手處做將去。自煉
精始，精住則然後煉氣，氣定則然後煉神，神凝則然後還虛，虛
之又虛，道德乃俱。

What I said above is only a general approximation of the Golden
Elixir. Just by looking at this, you will trust that the great undertak-
ing is not on paper. If this is not so, then you must know where to
set to practice. Once you know where to set to practice, start from
there and go ahead. Begin from refining Essence; when the Essence
is stabilized, refine the Breath; when the Breath is settled, refine the
Spirit; when the Spirit has coagulated, return to Emptiness. By being
empty and then again empty, Dao and virtue will be together.[60]

This chapter has explained some terms pertaining to what Li
Daochun calls "setting down to practice." A scale here, a claw there, and
one will be able to see the true principle.

[60] *Zhonghe ji*, chapter 3.

# 3　Refining Breath

# to Transmute it into Spirit

"Refining Essence to transmute it into Breath" is the "initial barrier." Essence is refined with Breath, and forms a Breath that becomes the "mother of the Elixir" (*danmu*). At this stage, "the Three return to the Two." In the next stage, "refining Breath to transmute it into Spirit," Breath is refined with Spirit, so that it returns to Spirit. At this stage, which is also called the "intermediate barrier," "the Two return to the One." After the "intermediate barrier," there will be only the One Spirit (*yishen*), and one will be able to progress to the "higher barrier."

The "intermediate barrier" is also called Barrier of the Ten Months (*shiyue guan*). The terms used to describe this stage include Great Medicine (*dayao*), Embryo of Sainthood (*shengtai*), "bathing at the four cardinal points" (*sizheng muyu*), "moving the tripod" (*yiding*), "going back and forth between the two Fields" (*ertian fanfu*), and Greater Celestial Circuit (*da zhoutian*). The Barrier of the Ten Months uses the metaphors of the ten-month pregnancy and the nurturing of the Numinous Medicine (*lingyao*). When the practice reaches this stage, it has already entered into its idealistic portion: it is deemed that if this stage of the practice is successful, one can invert the process of aging and return to youth, extend the length of one's life and obtain longevity.

However, although "refining Breath to transmute it into Spirit" abounds in ideals of a religious nature, it also involves arduous practice. The alchemical methods have evolved from the self-cultivation arts of the *fangshi* ("masters of the methods"); they are related to ancient medicine, but do not draw on the shamanic and mediumistic arts (*wushu*) and are not concerned with fictional discourses. The methods, nevertheless, are complex, and for this reason few practitioners reach this stage of inner refinement. But even when these practices to not attain full achievement, they are beneficial to the mind and the body; therefore I will introduce several relevant terms, with brief explications that may be consulted while reading the alchemical texts.

## The Great Medicine (dayao 大藥)

According to the principles of alchemy, between the stages of "refining Essence to transmute it into Breath" and "refining Breath to transmute it into Spirit" there is an intermediate stage. At that time, the Internal Medicine and the External Medicine coagulate with one another. First, by means of the external cycling of the Celestial Circuit, one accumulates the External Medicine; then, through the operation of Spirit, the External Medicine is moved to the lower Cinnabar Field and rapidly generates the Internal Medicine. When the Internal and the External Medicines coagulate and coalesce together in the lower Cinnabar Field, they form the Great Medicine (*dayao*). This is the so-called "mother of the Elixir" (*danmu*). After a further refining of seven days, which is called "entering the enclosure" (*ruhuan*), it forms the Embryo of Sainthood (*shengtai*), also called the Infant (*ying'er*). "Entering the enclosure" is also called "barrier of sitting" (*zuoguan*); in Buddhism, it is called "confinement" (*biguan*).[1]

## The Embryo of Sainthood (shengtai 聖胎)

In one of the poems quoted above, *Awakening to Reality* says:

三家相見結嬰兒，嬰兒是一含真氣，十月胎圓入聖基。

When the three families see one another,
the Infant coalesces.
The Infant is the One
holding True Breath;
in ten months the embryo is complete —
this is the foundation for entering sainthood.[2]

---

[1] On "entering the enclosure" see above, p. 69.
[2] *Wuzhen pian*, "Lüshi," poem 14.

Liu Yiming explains this poem as follows:

> 和合四象、攢簇五行，則精、氣、神凝結。是云三家相見，名曰嬰兒，又曰先天一氣，又曰聖胎，又曰金丹。

> When the four images join one another, and when the five agents gather together, then Essence, Breath, and Spirit coagulate and coalesce one with the other. Therefore it says "the three families see one another." This is called the Infant, the One Breath prior to Heaven, the Embryo of Sainthood, the Golden Elixir.[3]

Wu Shouyang says:

> 胎即神炁耳，非真有嬰兒也，非有形有象也。蓋大丹之成，先以神入乎其炁，後炁來包乎其神，如胎兒在胞中無呼吸又不能無呼吸，生滅之相尚在，出入之跡猶存，若胎孕之將產時，故比喻之曰懷胎、移胎、出胎。

> The Embryo is nothing but Spirit and Breath. It does not mean that there is truly an infant, or that it is something provided with a form and an image. Essentially, in the formation of the Great Elixir, first the Spirit enters the Breath, then the Breath is embraced by the Spirit. It is like an embryo in the womb: it does not breathe, but cannot live without breathing. Existence and extinction coexist in it with one another, coming and going are together in it with one another. It is like the coming to life of an actual embryo; this is why we use the metaphors of pregnancy (*huaitai*), "moving the embryo" (*yitai*), and delivery (*chutai*).[4]

The terms used by Wu Shouyang in this passage are metaphors for the return of Spirit to the state of "great stability" (*dading*) at this stage of the practice. With some exaggeration, the alchemical masters speak of "pregnancy in the middle Cinnabar Field" (*zhongtian huaitai*). The texts, however, never say that this should be understood in a literal way.

---

[3] Quoted, with some omissions, from Liu Yiming's *Wuzhen zhizhi*, "Lüshi," commentary to poem 14.

[4] This passage is not found in Wu Shouyang's *Tianxian zhengli zhilun*, which Wang Mu quotes as its source. A similar passage is found, however, in Wu Shouyang's *Xian Fo hezong yulu*, "Wu Taiyi shijiu wen," no. 6. On "moving the embryo" from the middle to the upper Cinnabar Field, see below, p. 112.

## "Bathing at the Four Cardinal Points" (sizheng muyu 四正沐浴)

The term "four cardinal points" (*sizheng*) refers to the four spatiotemporal markers Zi 子, Wu 午, Mao 卯, and You 酉, and to the four seasons, namely spring, summer, autumn, and winter (see table 8). Zi and Wu respectively correspond to North and South; their images in the precelestial arrangement of the trigrams are Qian ☰ and Kun ☷. Mao and You respectively correspond to East and West; their images in the precelestial arrangement of the trigrams are Kan ☵ and Li ☲. (See table 4.)

In addition, Zi, Wu, Mao, and You serve to mark the practice of "bathing" (*muyu*). The *Cantong qi* says:

> 子南午北，互為綱紀。
>
> Zi at South, Wu at North,
> are each other's guiding thread.[5]

It also says:

> 龍西虎東，建緯卯酉。
>
> Dragon at West, Tiger at East,
> across the way are Mao and You.[6]

In terms of locations, Zi is the Meeting of Yin (*huiyin*) cavity; Wu is the Palace of the Muddy Pellet (*niwan gong*); Mao is the Gate of Life (*mingmen*); and You is the Crimson Palace (*jianggong*).[7] In the Lesser Celestial Circuit, these are the locations of the "bathing at Mao and You" (*maoyou muyu*). In the Greater Celestial Circuit, they refer instead to the times of "bathing": since the Yang principle is born in the positions of these four cardinal points, one should innerly practice the method of "bathing" at the corresponding times.

In more detail, the difference between the "bathing" of the Lesser and the Greater Celestial Circuits is the following: In the Lesser Celestial Circuit, "bathing" consists in pausing Breath at the positions of Mao and

---

[5] *Cantong qi*, chapter 24. These verses allude to the "inversion" of the ordinary cosmological patterns, where Zi corresponds to the North and Wu corresponds to the South (see table 8).

[6] *Cantong qi*, chapter 24. These verses also allude to the principle of "inversion": ordinarily, the Dragon is an emblem of the East and the Tiger is an emblem of the West (see table 1).

[7] The Crimson Palace is the heart, or the central Cinnabar Field.

You. In the Greater Celestial Circuit, instead, one does not perform the circulation of the River Chariot: the murky and misty Original Breath stays between the Yellow Court and the Cinnabar Field. At that time, "bathing" consists in "washing the mind and cleansing the thoughts," steaming them with the True Breath, observing subtle silence and brightness with the eyes, and preventing the mind from wandering around unrestrained and becoming unstable.

Therefore, although there are set times, there are no set times.[8] As we have seen, Zhang Boduan says in his *Four Hundred Words on the Golden Elixir*:

火候不用時，冬至不在子，及其沐浴法，卯酉時虛比。

The Fire Times have no times,
the winter solstice is not at Zi (子);
and as for the method of bathing,
the times of Mao and You are empty similitudes.[9]

This means that the "four cardinal points" should be used in a flexible way: one should neither be mired in the images nor attached to the words, and should not be bound by either images or words. Zhongli Quan said: "When you bathe for one year, defend yourself from dangers."[10] "One year" is a conventional term; it refers to the four seasons, but also alludes to the "four cardinal points": autumn corresponds to the East, summer to the South, autumn to the West, and winter to the North. Within this context, the practice of "bathing" should be performed in a flexible way. However, there should not be excesses, and one should not let one's mind wander, for as soon as thoughts run unrestrained, dangers occur. The *Four Hundred Words on the Golden Elixir* says:

沐浴防危險，抽添自謹持，都來三萬刻，差失恐毫釐。

---

[8] This sentence is translated as literally as possible (the Chinese text is 「雖有定時,亦無定時」). Wang Mu says that "there are set times" because Zi, Wu, Mao, and You represent the cycle of time; but "there are no set times" because in this practice Zi, Wu, Mao, and You not only do not represent space (unlike the Lesser Celestial Circuit, which requires a spatial orientation), but they also do not represent time since, as Wang Mu has just explained, time per se is not involved in this practice.

[9] *Jindan sibai zi*, poem 13.

[10] This sentence is attributed to Zhongli Quan in several sources, e.g., Wu Shouyang's *Tianxian zhengli zhilun*, chapter 4.

When bathing, defend yourself from dangers,
When lessening and augmenting, carefully guard yourself.
Altogether there are thirty thousand periods:
watch for even the slightest mistake.[11]

This poem warns once more that, during the practice of "bathing at the four cardinal points," one should not let one's mind wander.

In the Greater Celestial Circuit, "bathing" uses "constancy" (chang). In the same spirit of the Daode jing, which says, "Constantly having no intentions, you observe its marvels; constantly having intentions, you observe its boundaries,"[12] in "bathing" there are constant stability and constant awareness. Once again, this differs from the "bathing" of the Lesser Celestial Circuit: by virtue of constant stability the thoughts appear to cease, and by virtue of constant awareness one should practice in accordance with "four cardinal points." However, this practice consists in inner contemplation (neiguan), and under this respect it is not different from the pausing at Mao and You that occurs in the Lesser Celestial Circuit.

*Awakening to Reality* says:

> 兔雞之月及其時，刑德臨門藥象之，到此金丹宜沐浴，若還加火
> 必傾危。

> As the months of the hare and the rooster reach their time,
> punishment and virtue approach the gates — the Medicine takes
>     these images as models.
> When you came to this, the Golden Elixir should be bathed:
> if you again increase the fire, you will be in danger.[13]

Mao and the hare correspond to the spring equinox and to Wood; since they are the life-giving Breath, they are called "virtue" (de). You and the rooster correspond to the autumn equinox and to Metal; since they are the life-taking Breath, they are called "punishment" (xing). All these terms refer to the positions of the "four cardinal points." "The Medicine takes these images as models" means that the emblems of the Medicine are Mao-Wood and You-Metal. At these times, therefore, one should stay in quiescence, perform inner observation, and steam the "mother of the Elixir" (danmu) by means of the True Breath. Cui Xifan's *Ruyao jing* says:

---

[11] *Jindan sibai zi*, poem 19.
[12] *Daode jing*, 1.
[13] *Wuzhen pian*, "Jueju," poem 34.

初結胎，看本命，終脫胎，看四正。

At the beginning coalesce the embryo:
observe your fundamental destiny.
At the end deliver the embryo:
observe the four cardinal points.[14]

This poem enunciates the same important point.

## The Greater Celestial Circuit (da zhoutian 大周天)

Seven days after the Great Medicine has been obtained, the barriers are cleared and one enters the stage of "refining Breath to transmute it into Spirit." I will describe below the difference between the Greater and the Lesser Celestial Circuits.

In the Lesser Celestial Circuit, the External Medicine is collected and is moved to the lower Cinnabar Field by means of the River Chariot: it passes through the tripod above (the Palace of the Muddy Pellet), reaches the stove below (the Cinnabar Field), and is sealed there in order to be preserved. The sinciput is called Qian-Tripod (qianding), and the lower Cinnabar Field is called Kun-Stove (kunlu).

In the Greater Celestial Circuit, instead, the tripod is moved below: the Yellow Court is the tripod, and the lower Cinnabar Field is the stove. The Original Breath, murky and misty, simply stays in the empty space between the two Fields; it should be guarded in that space, instead of being firmly held within one of the two Fields.

When one allows this to occur in a natural and flexible way, and by preserving a state of inaction, the Numinous Radiance (lingguang) will not be extinguished. This is actually the practice of "entering stability" (ruding), in which one proceeds from "doing" (youwei) to "non-doing" (wuwei). "Breath" itself proceeds from subtle movement to non-movement, and is exhausted and transmuted. The operation of the True Intention (zhenyi) also advances from the eyes' faculty of sight to a state of non-perception (wujue).

A poem of Awakening to Reality alludes to this state by saying:

[14] Ruyao jing, in Xiuzhen shishu, chapter 13.

果生枝上終期熟，子在胞中豈有殊。

A fruit grows on the branches
and ripens at the end of season:
could the Child in the womb
be different from this?[15]

An oral instruction on the alchemical practice says:

三萬刻中無間斷，行行坐坐轉分明。

Throughout thirty thousand periods there is no interval:
walking or sitting, you constantly revolve the Light.[16]

These words show that the Greater Celestial Circuit is not based on the cycling of Breath. It uses, instead, the function of subtle silence and brightness and the force of "entering stability" in order to allow the Original Spirit to grow and develop.

## The "True Zi Hour" (zheng zishi 正子時)

"Refining Essence and transmuting it into Breath" uses the "living Zi hour" (*huo zishi*). Despite the reference to the Zi hour, this is actually a code name to mean the time of the refining of the Medicine. Cui Xifan's *Ruyao jing* says:

一日內，十二辰，意所到，皆可為。

Within the day,
during the twelve hours,
wherever the Intention goes,
all can be done.[17]

---

[15] *Wuzhen pian*, "Lüshi," poem 5.
[16] *Xian Fo hezong yulu*, "Shouzhong."
[17] *Ruyao jing*, in *Xiuzhen shishu*, chapter 13. According to Xiao Tingzhi's commentary, these verses concerns to the possibility of performing the Neidan practice without regard to rules concerning time.

This is unrelated to time: at the stage of "refining Breath to transmute it into Spirit," the Great Medicine has already been formed, and thus there is no need to return to the "living Zi hour." When one produces the Great Medicine, therefore, the "living Zi hour" is not the time between 11 PM and 1 AM, which is ordinarily meant by the Zi hour. "True Zi hour" denotes, instead, a state or a condition; one could call it a sign that the Great Medicine has been completed. At this time, as the alchemical texts say, the Cinnabar Field blazes, the kidneys swelter, the eyes emit a golden light, the wind blows behind the ears, the eagles cry behind the brain, the body bubbles, and the nose twitches. All this means that the time of the Great Medicine has come; and this is what is called the "true Zi hour." The next step consists in allowing the Great Medicine to enter the Cinnabar Field, where it coagulates into the Elixir.

The stage of "refining Breath to transmute it into Spirit" constitutes an advanced stage of the alchemical work, in which one's practice progresses from "doing" to "non-doing." The Great Medicine is called Embryo of Sainthood (*shengtai*) or Infant (*ying'er*). Both terms are actually metaphors for Spirit and Breath coagulating and coalescing with one another. Wu Shouyang explains the meaning of these terms saying:

> 夫即喻之曰胎，宜若真似有胎矣，雖曰似胎，而實非胎也。何也？生人之理，胎嬰在腹;修仙之理，胎神在心。世人但聞胎之名，而遂謂腹中實有一嬰兒出，而為身外身者，實可笑也。蓋人性至虛至靈，無形無體。

> Metaphorically it is called "embryo," as if there is truly an embryo. In fact, however, there is no embryo. Why is it so? Because according to the principle of giving birth, one generates the embryo of a child in the womb; and according to the principle of cultivating immortality, one generates an embryo of Spirit in the Heart. The worldly people hear the word "embryo" and say that within the womb there is truly an embryo, which then leaves and becomes "a body outside the body" (*shen wai shen*). This is truly risible. Essentially, the human nature is perfectly empty and perfectly numinous; it is devoid of a form and a body.[18]

Wu Shouyang was a heir of the alchemical methods of the Southern and Northern lineages. Although he was an eighth-generation disciple of Qiu Chuji's (1148–1227) Northern Lineage, he did not reject the teachings of

---

[18] *Xian Fo hezong yulu*, "Wu Taiyi shijiu wen," no. 6 (with minor omissions and changes).

Zhang Boduan's *Awakening to Reality* and *Secret Text of Green Florescence.* Therefore the explanation of the embryo quoted above elaborates on the views of *Awakening to Reality.*

# 4　Refining Spirit
## to Return to Emptiness

"Refining Spirit to return to Emptiness" is the highest ideal of the alchemical doctrines. This stage is also called Higher Barrier (*shangguan*)
and Barrier of the Nine Years (*jiunian guan*). The term "nine years" does
not refer to the time required to achieve the Great Elixir; it alludes,
instead, to the story of Bodhidharma who sat facing a wall for nine years,
taking this as a metaphor for the stage in which one enters the practice
of Xing (Nature). In constant stability and constant silence, all things
return to the Origin. Therefore another name of this stage is "refining
Spirit to join with the Dao" (*lianshen hedao*), where Dao means Emptiness
and Non-Being (*xuwu*).

*Awakening to Reality* says:

> 道自虛無生一氣，便從一氣產陰陽，陰陽再合成三體，三體重生
> 萬物張。
>
> The Dao from Emptiness and Non-Being generates the One Breath,
> then from the One Breath gives birth to Yin and Yang;
> Yin and Yang join again and form the three bodies,
> the three bodies repeatedly generate, and the ten thousand things
>     grow.[1]

This poem describes the process of generation from the Dao, which is a
forward process of "going along" (or "continuing transformation,"
*shunhua*). The alchemical practice, instead, emphasizes the backward
process of "inverting the course" (*nixing*). It upholds that, in the first
place, "the three bodies return to two bodies," when Essence, Breath, and
Spirit are refined into Spirit and Breath; this is the stage of "refining
Essence to transmute it into Breath." Then comes the stage in which "the

---

[1]　*Wuzhen pian*, "Jueju," poem 12.

two bodies return to one body" and there is only the Original Spirit; this is the stage of "refining Breath to transmute it into Spirit." Finally comes "refining the One to revert to Non-Being" (*lianyi huanwu*), which is the stage of "refining Spirit to return to Emptiness."

As shown by the explanation given in the poem quoted above, "reverting to Emptiness and Non-Being" is equivalent to "returning to the Dao." Therefore the alchemical texts often use the symbol ○ to represent Emptiness—the state in which all things enter Emptiness and become entirely clear. One reverts to the fundament and returns to the root, enlightens one's mind and sees one's Nature. This is the highest goal of *Awakening to Reality*.

*Zhang Boduan and Buddhism.* According to the alchemical methods of Zhang Boduan, one should first cultivate one's Ming (Life) and then one's Xing (Nature), and should first devote oneself to the practices and then to the Way. In his preface to the *Wuzhen pian shiyi* (Supplement to *Awakening to Reality*), Zhang Boduan says:

> 『悟真篇』者，先以神仙命脈誘其修鍊，次以諸佛妙用廣其神通，終以真如覺性遣其幻妄，而歸於究竟空寂之本源矣。

> *Awakening to Reality* first attracts one to the practice of self-cultivation in accordance with the bloodline of the divine Immortals; then broadens one's spiritual comprehension in accordance with the wondrous operation of all the Buddhas; and finally leads one away from illusions and delusions in accordance with one's own true enlightened Nature. Thus one returns to the ultimate fundament of absolute emptiness and silence.[2]

As shown by this passage, when Zhang Boduan describes the fourth and highest stage of the alchemical practice, he uses Buddhist principles to explicate the "return to Emptiness." This differs from both the *Cantong qi* and the *Ruyao jing*. Opening a new path, Zhang Boduan employed Chan as a metaphor for the Dao. Although the respective ways of argumentation are different, his foundation was explaining the Taoist alchemical practice of Xing. In order to widen the vision of his disciples, therefore, he used metaphors of all kinds, and explained the profound meaning of "returning to Emptiness" by means of the Buddhist idea of the "true enlightened Nature."

---

[2] *Wuzhen pian shiyi*, Preface.

Between the late Tang and the Five Dynasties (ca. ninth-tenth centuries), the notion of the "unity of the Three Teachings" (*sanjiao heyi*) favored the integration and harmonization of Taoism, Confucianism, and Buddhism. During the Northern Song period (960–1127), the trend toward convergence continued: each of the Three Teachings was explicated by means of the others, and each drew from the others. Zhang Boduan himself was a disciple of Taoism who came from Confucianism and was also engaged in Buddhism. In his preface to *Awakening to Reality* he says:

> 僕幼親善道，涉獵三教經書，以至刑法、書、算、醫、卜、戰陣、天文、地理、吉凶、死生之術，靡不留心詳究。

> Since my youth, I have cherished the good Dao. I have inquired into the scriptures of the Three Teachings, and have also made careful and detailed studies of law, calligraphy, mathematics, medicine, divination, military science, astronomy, geography, prognostication, and the arts of life and death.[3]

As we can see from this passage, Zhang Boduan was well-versed in the principles of the Three Teachings, and was extremely learned. However, he was ultimately a master of the Taoist Golden Elixir, and he did not convert to Buddhism. During the Qing dynasty, the Yongzheng Emperor (r. 1723–35) issued an edict stating that Zhang Boduan had deeply understood the principles of Chan Buddhism. The emperor gave orders to incorporate *Awakening to Reality* into the Buddhist Canon and into the *Yuxuan yulu* (Imperial Compilation of Recorded Sayings).[4] He also granted Zhang Boduan the title of "Chan Immortal" (*chanxian*). All this was due to the emperor's own study of the Chan principles and to his adherence to those teachings. In fact, the principles of the Pure Cultivation branch (Qingxiu pai) of Taoist alchemy are in agreement with the Chan doctrine of "enlightening one's mind and seeing one's Nature" (*mingxin jianxing*). Therefore Zhang Boduan certainly drew from the Chan doctrine. However, his essential intent was to elucidate the profound meaning of "refining one's Nature" (*lianxing*). He was not both a Taoist and Buddhist, and in the appellation "Chan Immortal," the emphasis should fall on the word "immortal." In his preface to the *Yuxuan yulu*, the Yongzheng Emperor maintains that the three religions (Taoism, Confucianism, and

---

[3] *Wuzhen pian*, in *Xiuzhen shishu*, chapter 26, preface.

[4] The *Yuxuan yulu* (chapter 10 in the edition of the Buddhist Canon of the Qing period, the *Qianlong Dazang jing*), contains selections from the "Outer Chapters" of the *Wuzhen pian*.

Buddhism) are one, but this only reflects his own views on religion and government.

*Returning to Emptiness.* When the Zhong-Lü alchemical tradition explains "refining Spirit to return to Emptiness," it builds in the first place on the foundation of "refining Breath to transmute it into Spirit." One should move the Infant from the lower to the middle Cinnabar Field, where it is further refined and nourished. Then the Infant is moved from the middle to the upper Cinnabar Field; this is called "moving the embryo" (*yitai*). Finally one obtains the Yang Spirit, which exits from the Gate of Heaven (*tianmen*); this is called "delivery of the embryo" (*chutai*), and is also called "nourishing warmly" (*wenyang*). This is not mentioned in any of Zhang Boduan's works. *Awakening to Reality* says:

> 藥逢氣類方成象，道在希夷合自然，一粒靈丹吞入腹，始知我命不由天。

> Only when the Medicines meet in breath (*qi*) and kind do they form an image:
> the Dao is inaudible and invisible, and is joined to What is so by Itself.
> Ingest the one grain of numinous Elixir, let it enter the belly,
> and for the first time you will know that your destiny does not depend on Heaven.[5]

This poem refers the *Daode jing*, which says: "Look at it, and you do not see it: it is called invisible. Listen to it, and you do not hear it: it is called inaudible."[6] As one dwells in constant stability and constant silence, and is pervasive in responding to the external impulses, the four elements return to emptiness, and one escapes from the cycle of birth and death.[7] Zhang Boduan does not explain the "egress of the Yang Spirit" (*chu yangshen*) and other imaginary states, but considers "returning to Emptiness" to be the same as purely entering non-doing, being entirely pervasive and unhindered, being existent for ever and ever like Heaven and Earth, and obtaining the Great Liberation (*da jietuo*).

---

[5] *Wuzhen pian*, "Jueju," poem 54.

[6] *Daode jing*, 14.

[7] In Buddhism, the four elements (*sida*), namely Earth, Water, Fire, and Wind, are respectively related to the qualities of hardness, wetness, warming, and movement. Their joining gives birth to the material entities.

A poem in the "Outer Chapters" ("Waipian") of *Awakening to Reality* says:

法法法元無法，空空空亦非空，靜喧語默本來同，夢裏何勞說夢。有用用中無用，無功功裏施功，還如果熟自然紅，莫問如何修種。

> The dharma makes the dharma into the dharma—originally there is
>     no dharma;
> and when emptiness empties emptiness—then it not emptiness.
> Quiescence and noise, speech and silence are fundamentally the
>     same:
> while in a dream, why trouble yourself with talking of the dream?
> In operation, within the operation there is no operation;
> in non-function, within the function arises the function.
> It is like a fruit that ripens, and of its own its color turns to red:
> never ask how to cultivate the seed.[8]

This is the true meaning of "refining Spirit to return to Emptiness" in *Awakening to Reality*. Another poem in the "Outer Chapters" says:

如來妙體遍河沙，萬象森羅無礙遮，會得圓通真法眼，始知三界是吾家。

> The wondrous body of the Tathagata is as manifold as the sands of
>     the Ganges;
> the ten thousand phenomena, interminable and unceasing, are
>     unhindered and unconcealed.
> If you understand the true Eye of the Dharma, which pervades every
>     thing,
> for the first time you will know that the three worlds are your
>     home.[9]

This view of the "return to Emptiness" is the same as the view of Chan Buddhism. Therefore the final state of realization is the same in both teachings. Weng Baoguang explains this point saying:

---

[8]  *Wuzhen pian*, "Waipian," "Xijiang yue," poem 4. In the first line, the word *fa* can also mean "model," and the line could also be rendered: "The model models itself on the model—originally there is no model."

[9]  *Wuzhen pian*, "Waipian," "Jueju," poem 1.

九載功圓，則無為之性自圓，無形之神自妙，神妙則變化無窮，
隱顯莫測；性圓則慧照十方，靈通無破。故能分身百億，應顯無
方，而其至真之體，處於至靜之域，寂然而未嘗有作者，此其神
性形命俱與道合真矣。

When the nine-year practice is concluded, in its non-doing, one's
Nature is of its own perfect, and in its formlessness, one's Spirit is of
its own wondrous. When Spirit is wondrous, is transformations are
inexhaustible, and its states of manifestation and non-manifestation
are unfathomable. When Nature is perfect, its wisdom illuminates
all directions, and in its being numinous and pervasive, it can suffer
no damage. Therefore one can can divide one's being into a myriad
beings that manifest themselves in limitless ways, while one's own
body of utmost reality dwells in the realm of utmost quiescence,
silent and ceaselessly abiding in non-doing. This is because one's
Nature, one's Spirit, one's form, and one's existence are joined in
their reality with the reality of the Dao.[10]

This is the ideal of "returning to Emptiness" in *Awakening to Reality*. The
"Outer Chapters" describe it with a metaphor:

我有一輪明鏡，從來只為蒙昏，今朝磨瑩照乾坤，萬象昭然難
隱。

I have a round bright mirror,
it has always been muddied.
Today I rub it and polish it, so that it may reflect Qian and Kun:
the ten thousand phenomena are clear, and can hardly hide themselves.[11]

In this state there is no concealment and no hindrance. The ten thousand
images are entirely luminous; they join as one with Heaven and Earth,
and form a single body with the entire cosmos.

*Body and Spirit.* However, Zhang Boduan belongs to the Taoist alchemical
tradition, and his approach to the question of form and spirit differs from
Buddhism. The goal of Buddhist self-cultivation is crossing to the "other
shore," "undergoing reincarnation," and obtaining "ultimate bliss
through rebirth." The corporeal frame is seen as a temporary lodge.
Taoism, instead, maintains that form and spirit should be in agreement

---

[10] *Wuzhen zhizhi xiangshuo sansheng biyao*, "Shenxian baoyi zhi Dao."
[11] *Wuzhen pian*, "Waipian," "Xijiang yue," poem 2.

with one another, so that one may extend the length of one's life. The Yang Spirit (*yangshen*) can leave the body, but after one thousand or ten thousand transformations it can re-enter the corporeal frame. The highest ideal is ascending to Heaven in one's tangible body, or even "raising in flight with one's entire family." And although Taoism mentions the "winged transformation" (*yuhua*) and the "liberation from the corpse" (*shijie*), the corporeal frame that is discarded is not the actual physical body, and those are illusory transformations.[12]

Zhang Boduan does not provide many details on this point, but his poems often refer to the agreement of body and spirit. One of them says, for example:

> 只候功成朝北闕，九霞光裏駕翔鸞。
>
> Just wait until your work is achieved
> to have audience at the Northern Portal,
> and in the radiance of a ninefold mist
> you will ride a soaring phoenix.[13]

Another poem says:

> 已知壽永齊天地，煩惱無由更上心。
>
> Once you know that your longevity
> equals that of Heaven and Earth,
> troubles and vexations have no way
> to rise to your heart.[14]

Another poem says:

> 群陰消盡丹成熟，跳出凡籠壽萬年。
>
> When all of Yin is entirely dispelled,
> the Elixir ripens:
> you leap out of the cage of the mundane,
> and live ten thousand years.[15]

---

[12] The term "winged transformation" alludes to the ancient representations of the immortals as beings provided with wings and feathers that enable them to fly to Heaven. "Release from the corpse" is a form of simulated death that allows an adept to leave his mortal body, and replace it with a perfected body that enables him to continue his practice until final liberation.

[13] *Wuzhen pian*, "Lüshi," poem 3.

[14] *Wuzhen pian*, "Lüshi," poem 10.

[15] *Wuzhen pian*, "Lüshi," poem 13.

And again:

> 萬物芸芸各返根，返根復命即常存。
>
> The ten thousand things, in all their multiplicity, return to the root;
> as they return to the root and revert to life, they are constantly
> preserved.[16]

All the poems quoted above show that Zhang Boduan agrees with the
Taoist views on attaining long life.

On the other hand, Zhang Boduan dissents from the Buddhist views
on reincarnation. In another poem, he says:

> 饒君了悟真如性，未免抛身卻入身，何似更兼修大藥，頓超無漏
> 作真人。
>
> Even if you awaken to your own true enlightened Nature,
> you have not yet escaped reincarnation.
> How about also cultivating the Great Medicine,
> so that you may immediately transcend to the uncontaminated
> state and become a True Man?[17]

This poem alludes to the Buddhist separation and duality of form and
spirit. In the Taoist Golden Elixir, instead, Reality is achieved by means of
"refining the form" (*lianxing*). Therefore Zhang Boduan says in another
poem:

> 釋氏教人修極樂，只緣極樂是金方，大都色相惟茲實，餘者非真
> 漫度量。
>
> Buddhism teaches people to cultivate ultimate bliss:
> just following ultimate bliss is the direction of Metal.
> Within all forms and phenomena, only this is real—
> anything else is unreal and vain to assay.[18]

"Direction of Metal" (*jinfang*) has a double meaning: in the first meaning,
it represents the West, and in the second one, it represents the Golden
Elixir.

---

[16] *Wuzhen pian*, "Jueju," poem 51.

[17] *Wuzhen pian*, "Qiyan jueju," poem 1. "Uncontaminated" translates *wulou*, the
Chinese term for *anāsrava*.

[18] *Wuzhen pian*, "Qiyan jueju," poem 4.

After the Golden Elixir has been achieved, it cannot be damaged or extinguished, and it is preserved for as long as Heaven and Earth. This is the "real form" or phenomenon alluded to by Zhang Boduan in the poem quoted above. Therefore Liu Yiming, in his commentary on *Awakening to Reality*, induces his disciples to engage themselves in Buddhism; when he discusses the true enlightened Nature, however, his explanation differs from Buddhism.

Although the "Outer Chapters" ("Waipian") of *Awakening to Reality* illustrate the notion of True Nature by means of Buddhist principles, they ultimately consist of a conclusion concerned with the highest ideals of Taoism. It is precisely for this reason, in fact, that the portion of Zhang Boduan's work containing poems on Chan principles is entitled "Outer Chapters." The Yongzheng Emperor of the Qing dynasty made Buddhism the national religion, intending to use Buddhism to restrain the Mongols and the Tibetans, and Taoism to control the Han ethnic groups. This is why he bestowed the title of "Chan Immortal" onto Zhang Boduan, and included his work into the Buddhist Canon. His political skills did not go much beyond using religion to attain his own goals.

In conclusion, "refining Spirit to return to Emptiness" lies in entering the pure practice of Xing (Nature). Although this practice may involve fantasies of a religious nature, for *Awakening to Reality* it only consists in progressing from delusion to awakening, and from awakening to Reality.

Part 3

# CONCLUSION

# The "Arts of the Way"

The Taoist "arts of the Way" (*daoshu*) derive from two sources. The first is the shamanic and mediumistic arts (*wushu*), which involve such practices as the use of talismans, spells, prayers, and planchette writing (*fuji*). The second is the self-cultivation arts of the *fangshi* ("masters of the methods"), which include breathing, diets, and so forth. Originally, both types of arts were subsumed under the denomination of "arts of the Way" (*daoshu*). From the late Tang period onward, Neidan gradually began to attract attention. The Pure Cultivation branch (Qingxiu pai) also admitted certain Buddhist principles, which were integrated into the alchemical practice. Zhang Boduan gathered the achievements of several masters; these provided the foundations for the principles of the Internal Elixir in his *Awakening to Reality*, which he deemed to represent the core of the "arts of the Way."

The author of *Awakening to Reality* entered Taoism coming from Confucianism, and also studied the Classics and the historical texts. His learning was broad and deep, and he widely sought teachers and companions. Therefore his alchemical methods give emphasis to the practical aspects. He recommends arduous practice, and is neither interested in fictional discourses nor concerned with speeches by gods or spirits. He only advocates nourishing the Three Treasures and controlling the body and the mind. He intends to probe into the ultimate origin of life and to indicate a path for self-cultivation.

In addition to understanding the principles of medicine, Zhang Boduan also studied astronomy and geography. His *Book of the Eight Vessels* was incorporated by Li Shizhen in his *Bencao gangmu*, and is an invaluable source for the study of traditional Chinese medicine. His methods for the initial stage of the practice and for "refining Essence and transmuting it into Breath" have been used for present-day research into the healing methods of Qigong. Zhang Boduan did emphasize the practices of "ceasing thoughts," "harmonizing the breathing," "using the Intention as a guide," and "clearing the Barriers"; all these practices, however, are closely related to medicine and healing, and thus can be seen as a precious legacy on the value of "sitting in quiescence" for healing purposes.

Needless to say, Zhang Boduan was a Taoist adept, and could hardly refrain from adopting a religious, mystical, or idealistic way of seeing. In his *Secret Text of Green Florescence*, however, he maintains that "the Heart is the lord; Spirit is the ruler; and the Intention is the go-between." In practice, this means that the Heart is the material foundation of the brain; the Spirit is the function of the brain; and the Intention is the activity of the brain. Although Zhang Boduan also emphasizes harmonizing the functions of vitality and thoughts, he actually assigns them a secondary rank.

Concerning his investigations into the origins of life, Zhang Boduan emphasizes that the "Medicine" is a function of Essence, Breath, and Spirit that coagulate with one another. His view that Essence is the foundation of life, and his method of using the Intention to lead the cyclical movement of the True Breath within the body, are consistent with the constitution of the human body, and avail themselves of the principles of self-healing that are inborn in the human being. Zhang Boduan's attitude of carrying out a deep investigation into the origins of life in order to attain longevity, as well as his notion that human life is related to the movements of Heaven and Earth, contain elements of the candid materialism that is also seen in the ancient Chinese philosophy of life. He developed the principles of the ancient alchemical classic, the *Cantong qi*, and integrated them with Buddhist principles concerning the cultivation of one's Nature. Moreover, he assimilated various ancient methods of Nourishing Life, including *daoyin*, inner observation, embryonic breathing, and meditation, into his own alchemical methods. These methods are pragmatic, and do not rely on pointless discourses; they collect the heritage of traditional medicine, and recapitulate the methods of healing and long life elaborated by the ancient Chinese people.

For those who study these subjects in the present day and will study them in the future, Zhang Boduan's work is invaluable not only as a source that enables us to investigate the philosophy of life, but also as a legacy that allows us to probe into life's very own secret.

Tables

# Table 1: Five Agents (Associations)

| | WOOD | FIRE | SOIL | METAL | WATER |
|---|---|---|---|---|---|
| DIRECTIONS | east | south | center | west | north |
| SEASONS | spring | summer | (midsummer) | autumn | winter |
| COLORS | green | red | yellow | white | black |
| EMBLEMATIC ANIMALS | green dragon | vermilion sparrow | yellow dragon | white tiger | snake and turtle |
| NUMBERS | 3, 8 | 2, 7 | 5, 10 | 4, 9 | 1, 6 |
| YIN-YANG (1) | minor Yang | great Yang | balance | minor Yin | great Yin |
| YIN-YANG (2) | True Yin | Yang | balance | True Yang | Yin |
| STEMS | *jia* 甲 *yi* 乙 | *bing* 丙 *ding* 丁 | *wu* 戊 *ji* 己 | *geng* 庚 *xin* 辛 | *ren* 壬 *gui* 癸 |
| BRANCHES | *yin* 寅 *mao* 卯 | *wu* 午 *si* 巳 | *xu* 戌, *chou* 丑 *wei* 未, *chen* 辰 | *you* 酉 *shen* 申 | *hai* 亥 *zi* 子 |
| PLANETS | Jupiter | Mars | Saturn | Venus | Mercury |
| RELATIONS | father | daughter | ancestors | mother | son |
| VISCERA | liver | heart | spleen | lungs | kidneys |
| BODY ORGAN | eyes | tongue | mouth | nose | ears |

Table 1. The five agents (*wuxing*) and their associations.

# Table 2: Five Agents (Spatial Distribution)

FIRE
South
Vermilion Sparrow
2
cinnabar
Original Spirit (*yuanshen* 元神)

| WOOD | SOIL | METAL |
|------|------|-------|
| East | Center | West |
| Green Dragon | | White Tiger |
| 3 | 5 | 4 |
| True Mercury | | True Lead |
| inner nature (*xing* 性) | intention (*yi* 意) | qualities (*qing* 情) |

WATER
North
Dark Warrior
1
black lead
Original Essence (*yuanjing* 元精)

Table 2. Spatial arrangement of the five agents (*wuxing*), with some of their main associations. In agreement with the traditional Chinese convention, North is shown at the bottom, South at the top, East on the left, and West on the right.

# Table 3: Eight Trigrams (Associations)

| ☰ | ☱ | ☲ | ☳ | ☴ | ☵ | ☶ | ☷ |
|---|---|---|---|---|---|---|---|
| 乾 | 兌 | 離 | 震 | 巽 | 坎 | 艮 | 坤 |
| QIAN | DUI | LI | ZHEN | XUN | KAN | GEN | KUN |
| heaven | lake | fire | thunder | wind | water | mountain | earth |
| father | youngest daughter | second daughter | eldest son | eldest daughter | second son | youngest son | mother |
| south | southeast | east | northeast | southwest | west | northwest | north |
| northwest | west | south | east | southeast | north | northeast | southwest |

Table 3. The eight trigrams (*bagua*) and their main associations.
From top to bottom: elements in nature, family relations,
and directions in the cosmological configurations
"prior to Heaven" (*xiantian*) and "posterior to Heaven" (*houtian*).

# Table 4: Eight Trigrams (Spatial Distribution)

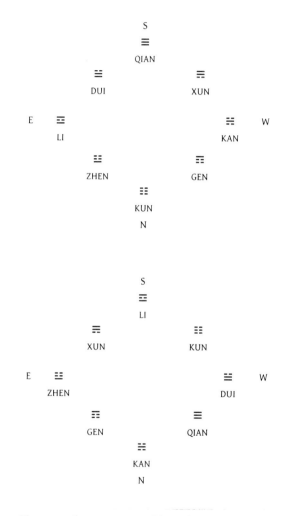

Table 4. Spatial arrangements of the eight trigrams (*bagua*)
in the cosmological configurations "prior to Heaven" (*xiantian*, top)
and "posterior to Heaven" (*houtian*, bottom).

# Table 5: Sixty Hexagrams

| | DAYTIME | | | NIGHTTIME |
|---|---|---|---|---|
| 1 | Zhun 屯 ䷂ | | ䷃ | Meng 蒙 |
| 2 | Xu 需 ䷄ | | ䷅ | Song 訟 |
| 3 | Shi 師 ䷆ | | ䷇ | Bi 比 |
| 4 | Xiaoxu 小畜 ䷈ | | ䷉ | Lü 履 |
| 5 | Tai 泰 ䷊ | | ䷋ | Pi 否 |
| 6 | Tongren 同人 ䷌ | | ䷍ | Dayou 大有 |
| 7 | Qian 謙 ䷎ | | ䷏ | Yu 豫 |
| 8 | Sui 隨 ䷐ | | ䷑ | Gu 蠱 |
| 9 | Lin 臨 ䷒ | | ䷓ | Guan 觀 |
| 10 | Shike 噬嗑 ䷔ | | ䷕ | Bi 賁 |
| 11 | Bo 剝 ䷖ | | ䷗ | Fu 復 |
| 12 | Wuwang 無妄 ䷘ | | ䷙ | Dachu 大畜 |
| 13 | Yi 頤 ䷚ | | ䷛ | Daguo 大過 |
| 14 | Xian 咸 ䷞ | | ䷟ | Heng 恆 |
| 15 | Dun 遯 ䷠ | | ䷡ | Dazhuang 大壯 |
| 16 | Jin 晉 ䷢ | | ䷣ | Mingyi 明夷 |
| 17 | Jiaren 家人 ䷤ | | ䷥ | Kui 睽 |
| 18 | Juan 蹇 ䷦ | | ䷧ | Jie 解 |
| 19 | Sun 損 ䷨ | | ䷩ | Yi 益 |
| 20 | Guai 夬 ䷪ | | ䷫ | Gou 姤 |
| 21 | Cui 萃 ䷬ | | ䷭ | Sheng 升 |
| 22 | Kun 困 ䷮ | | ䷯ | Jing 井 |
| 23 | Ge 革 ䷰ | | ䷱ | Ding 鼎 |
| 24 | Zhen 震 ䷲ | | ䷳ | Gen 艮 |
| 25 | Jian 漸 ䷴ | | ䷵ | Guimei 歸妹 |
| 26 | Feng 豐 ䷶ | | ䷷ | Lü 旅 |
| 27 | Xun 巽 ䷸ | | ䷹ | Dui 兌 |
| 28 | Huan 渙 ䷺ | | ䷻ | Jie 節 |
| 29 | Zhongfu 中孚 ䷼ | | ䷽ | Xiaoguo 小過 |
| 30 | Jiji 既濟 ䷾ | | ䷿ | Weiji 未濟 |

Table 5. Sequence of the sixty hexagrams during the thirty days of the month. Qian ䷀, Kun ䷁, Kan ䷜, and Li ䷝ are not part of this cycle.

## Table 6: "Sovereign Hexagrams"

| ䷗ | ䷒ | ䷊ | ䷡ | ䷪ | ䷀ | ䷫ | ䷠ | ䷋ | ䷓ | ䷖ | ䷁ |
|---|---|---|---|---|---|---|---|---|---|---|---|
| 復 | 臨 | 泰 | 大壯 | 夬 | 乾 | 姤 | 遯 | 否 | 觀 | 剝 | 坤 |
| Fu | Lin | Tai | Dazhuang | Guai | Qian | Gou | Dun | Pi | Guan | Bo | Kun |

| 子 | 丑 | 寅 | 卯 | 辰 | 巳 | 午 | 未 | 申 | 酉 | 戌 | 亥 |
|---|---|---|---|---|---|---|---|---|---|---|---|
| zi | chou | yin | mao | chen | si | wu | wei | shen | you | xu | hai |

| 黃鐘 | 大呂 | 太簇 | 夾鐘 | 姑洗 | 仲呂 | 蕤賓 | 林鐘 | 夷則 | 南呂 | 無射 | 應鐘 |
|---|---|---|---|---|---|---|---|---|---|---|---|
| huangzhong | dalü | taicou | jiazhong | guxi | zhonglü | ruibin | linzhong | yize | nanlü | wuyi | yingzhong |

| 11 | 12 | 1 | 2 | 3 | 4 | 5 | 6 | 7 | 8 | 9 | 10 |
|---|---|---|---|---|---|---|---|---|---|---|---|
| 23–1 | 1–3 | 3–5 | 5–7 | 7–9 | 9–11 | 11–13 | 13–15 | 15–17 | 17–19 | 19–21 | 21–23 |

Table 6. The twelve "sovereign hexagrams" (*bigua*) and their relation to other duodenary series: earthly branches (*dizhi*), bells and pitch-pipes (*zhonglü*), months of the year, and "double hours" (*shi*).

# Table 7: Celestial Stems

| | STEMS | | AGENTS | DIRECTIONS | COLORS | VISCERA | NUMBERS |
|---|---|---|---|---|---|---|---|
| 1 | *jia* | 甲 | WOOD | east | green | liver | 3, 8 |
| 2 | *yi* | 乙 | | | | | |
| 3 | *bing* | 丙 | FIRE | south | red | heart | 2, 7 |
| 4 | *ding* | 丁 | | | | | |
| 5 | *wu* | 戊 | SOIL | center | yellow | spleen | 5 |
| 6 | *ji* | 己 | | | | | |
| 7 | *geng* | 庚 | METAL | west | white | lungs | 4, 9 |
| 8 | *xin* | 辛 | | | | | |
| 9 | *ren* | 壬 | WATER | north | black | kidneys | 1, 6 |
| 10 | *gui* | 癸 | | | | | |

Table 7. The ten celestial stems (*tiangan*) and their associations.

# Table 8: Earthly Branches

| | BRANCHES | | AGENTS | DIRECTIONS | HOURS | NUMBERS |
|---|---|---|---|---|---|---|
| 1 | *zi* | 子 | WATER | N | 23–1 | 1, 6 |
| 2 | *chou* | 丑 | SOIL | NNE 3/4 E | 1–3 | 5, 10 |
| 3 | *yin* | 寅 | WOOD | ENE 3/4 N | 3–5 | 3, 8 |
| 4 | *mao* | 卯 | WOOD | E | 5–7 | 3, 8 |
| 5 | *chen* | 辰 | SOIL | ESE 3/4 S | 7–9 | 5, 10 |
| 6 | *si* | 巳 | FIRE | SSE 3/4 E | 9–11 | 2, 7 |
| 7 | *wu* | 午 | FIRE | S | 11–13 | 2, 7 |
| 8 | *wei* | 未 | SOIL | SSW 3/4 W | 13–15 | 5, 10 |
| 9 | *shen* | 申 | METAL | WSW 3/4 S | 15–17 | 4, 9 |
| 10 | *you* | 酉 | METAL | W | 17–19 | 4, 9 |
| 11 | *xu* | 戌 | SOIL | WNW 3/4 N | 19–21 | 5, 10 |
| 12 | *hai* | 亥 | WATER | NNW 3/4 W | 21–23 | 1, 6 |

Table 8. The twelve earthly branches (*dizhi*) and their associations.

# Glossary of Chinese Characters

*anmo daoyin* 按摩導引 ("pressing and rubbing" and "guiding and pulling")

*anyin* 按引 ("pressing and pulling")

*bagua* 八卦 (eight trigrams)

Bai Yuchan 白玉蟾 (1194–1229?)

*bairi guan* 百日關 (Barrier of the Hundred Days)

*Baizi bei* 百字碑 (Hundred-Character Tablet)

*bamai* 八脈 (Eight Vessels)

*Bamai jing* 八脈經 (Book of the Eight Vessels)

*Baopu zi* 抱樸子 (Book of the Master Who Embraces Spontaneous Nature)

*baoyi* 抱一 (embracing Unity)

*beihai* 北海 (Northern Ocean)

Beizong 北宗 (Northern Lineage)

*Bencao gangmu* 本草綱目 (Pharmacopoeia Arranged into Headings and Subheadings)

*bi* 彼 (the "other")

*biguan* 閉關 (confinement)

*bixi* 閉息 (stopping breathing)

*cai* 採 ("gathering")

*canghai* 滄海 (Azure Sea)

*Cantong qi* 參同契 (Token for the Joining of the Three)

*Cantong qi chanyou* 參同契闡幽 (Clarification of Obscurities in the *Cantong qi*)

*Cantong zhizhi* 參同契直指 (Straightforward Directions on the *Cantong qi*)

*canxia* 餐霞 ("swallowing mist")

*chang* 常 (constancy)

*Changdao zhenyan* 唱道真言 (True Words Chanting the Dao)

*Changsheng quanjing* 長生詮經 (Book on the Principles of Long Life)

*changuan* 禪觀 (contemplation)

*chanxian* 禪仙 ("Chan Immortal")

Chen Niwan 陳泥丸 (?–1213)

Chen Tuan 陳摶 (ca. 920–89)

Chen Zhixu 陳致虛 (1290–ca. 1368)

*chengjiang xue* 承漿穴 (Receiver of Fluids cavity)

*chongmai* 衝脈 (Thoroughfare vessel)

*chu yangshen* 出陽神 ("egress of the Yang Spirit")

*chuguan* 初關 ("initial barrier")

*chutai* 出胎 ("delivery of the embryo")

*cuancu* 攢簇 ("gathering together")

Cui Xifan 崔希範 (ca. 880–940)

*da dinglu* 大鼎爐 (Great Tripod and Stove)

*da jietuo* 大解脫 (Great Liberation)

*da zhoutian* 大周天 (Greater Celestial Circuit)

*dadan* 大丹 (Great Elixir)

*dading* 大定 (great stability)

*daimai* 帶脈 (Girdle vessel)

*Dandao jiupian* 丹道九篇 (Nine Essays on the Way of the Elixir)

*danmu* 丹母 ("mother of the Elixir")

*dantian* 丹田 (Cinnabar Field)

*dantou* 丹頭 ("matrix of the Elixir")

*Danyang zhenren yulu* 丹陽真人語錄 (Recordes Sayings of the True Man Ma Danyang)

*Daode jing* 道德經 (Book of the Way and its Virtue)

*Daode jing zhushi* 道德經注釋 (Commentary and Exegesis to the *Book the Way and its Virtue*)

*daoshu* 道術 (arts of the Way)

*daotai* 道胎 (Embryo of the Dao)

*daoxin* 道心 ("mind of the Dao")

*daoyin* 導引 ("guiding and pulling")

*Daoyuan jingwei ge* 道源精微歌 (Delicate Songs on the Origins in the Dao)

*Daozang jinghua lu* 道藏精華錄 (Record of the Essential Splendors of the Taoist Canon)

*dayao* 大藥 (Great Medicine)

*de* 德 (virtue)

*dihu* 地戶 (Door of Earth)

Ding Fubao 丁福保 (1874–1952)

*Dinglu shi* 鼎爐詩 (Poem on the Tripod and the Stove)

*dizhi* 地支 (earthly branches)

*dongtai* 動態 (dynamic state)

*duiduan xue* 兌端穴 (Mouth Extremity cavity)

*dumai* 督脈 (Control vessel)

*dunfa* 頓法 ("immediate method")

*duo zaohua* 奪造化 ("stealing creation and transformation")

*ertian fanfu* 二田反復 ("going back and forth between the two Fields")

*fa* 法 (dharma; model)

*famen* 法門 (dharma-gate)

*fangen fuming* 返根復命 ("returning to the root and reverting to life")

*fangshi* 方士 ("masters of the methods")

*fenbi* 分泌 (internal secretions)

*fengfu xue* 風府穴 (Cavity of the Wind Palace)

Fu Jinquan 付金銓 (1765–1844)

*fuji* 扶乩 (planchette writing)

*fuming guan* 復命關 (Barrier of the Return to Life)

*fuqi* 服氣 ("ingesting breath")

*gangqi* 剛氣 ("firm breath")

*genqiao* 根竅 (Root-Opening)

*guan* 關 ("barriers")

*guanqiao* 關竅 (Opening of the Barrier)

*Guanwu jin* 觀物吟 (Chant on the Contemplation of Things)

*guigen fuming* 歸根復命 ("reverting to the root and returning to life")

*guixi* 龜息 ("breathing like a turtle")

*guizhong* 規中 (Center of the Compass)

Guo Qingfan 郭慶藩 (1844–96)

*gushen* 谷神 (Spirit of the Valley)

*heche* 河車 (River Chariot)

*Hetu* 河圖 (Chart of the Yellow River)

*hou* 候 ("times, periods, spans of time")

*houtian* 後天 (postcelestial, "posterior to Heaven")

*houtian jing* 後天精 (postcelestial essence)

*houtian qi* 後天氣 (postcelestial breath)

*houxi* 喉息 ("breathing through the throat")

*huan* 還 (return)

*huandan* 還丹 (Reverted Elixir)

*huandu* 環堵 (enclosure)

Huang Baijia 黃百家 (1643–1709)

*huangdao* 黃道 (Yellow Path)

*Huangdi neijing suwen* 黃帝內經素問 (Inner Book of the Yellow Emperor: The Plain Questions)

*Huanghu jin* 恍惚吟 ("Chang of the Vague and Indistinct")

*huangpo* 黃婆 (Yellow Dame)

*Huangting jing* 黃庭經 (Scripture of the Yellow Court)

*huangting xue* 黃庭穴 (Cavity of the Yellow Court)

*huangting* 黃庭 (Yellow Court)

*huanjing bunao* 還精補腦 ("reverting the course of the Essence to replenish the brain")

*Huanyuan pian* 還源篇 (Reverting to the Origin)

Huashan 華山 (Mount Hua)

*huiguang fanzhao* 回光返照 ("circulating the light and inverting the radiance")

*huiyin xue* 會陰穴 (Meeting of Yin cavity)

*huo bi jinxing* 火逼金行 ("Fire pressing Metal into movement")

*huo zishi* 活子時 ("living Zi hour")

*huohou* 火候 (Fire Times)

*huxi* 呼吸 ("respiration," "exhaling and inhaling")

*jiaji* 夾脊 (Spinal Handle)

*jianfa* 漸法 ("gradual method")

Jiang Weiqiao 蔣維喬 (1872–1955)

*jiaogan jing* 交感精 ("essence of the intercourse," i.e., semen)

*jin yanghuo* 進陽火 ("advancing the Yang Fire")

*jin* 斤 (pound)

*Jindan dacheng ji* 金丹大成集 (The Great Achievement of the Golden Elixir)

*Jindan dayao* 金丹大要 (Great Essentials of the Golden Elixir)

*Jindan sibai zi* 金丹四百字 (Four Hundred Words on the Golden Elixir)

*Jindan wenda* 金丹問答 (Questions and Answers on the Golden Elixir)

*jinfang* 金方 ("direction of Metal")

*jing* 精 (essence)

*jing* 靜 (quiescence)

*jingming xue* 睛明穴 (Eyes' Light cavity)

*jingzuo* 靜坐 ("sitting in quiescence")

*jinhuo tuifu* 進火退符 ("advancing the Fire and withdrawing in response")

*jinhuo* 進火 ("advancing the Fire")

*jinmen* 禁門 (Forbidden Gate)

*Jiqian ge* 繼前歌 (Song of Following the Antecedent)

*jiunian guan* 九年關 (Barrier of the Nine Years)

*jun* 君 (lord)

*keqi* 客氣 ("extraneous breaths")

*Kuaihuo ge* 快活歌 (Song of Joyful Life)

*kunlu* 坤爐 (Kun ☷ Stove)

Kunlun 崑崙

*lao fengbi* 牢封閉 ("sealing tightly")

Li Buye 李樸野 (Ming dynasty)

Li Daochun 李道純 (fl. ca. 1290)

Li Shizhen 李時珍 (1518–93)

Li Xiyue 李西月 (1806–56)

*liandao chengsheng* 煉道成聖 ("refining the Dao to achieve sainthood")

*liang* 兩 (ounce)

*lianjing huaqi* 煉精化炁 ("refining Essence to transmute it into Breath")

*lianming* 煉命 ("refining one's Life")

*lianqi huashen* 煉炁化神 ("refining Breath to transmute it into Spirit")

*lianshen hedao* 煉神合道 ("refining Spirit to join with the Dao")

*lianshen huanxu* 煉神還虛 ("refining Spirit to return to Emptiness")

*lianxing* 煉形 ("refining the form")

*lianxing* 煉性 ("refining one's Nature")

*lianxing huaqi* 煉形化炁 ("refining the form to transmute it into Breath")

*lianyi huanwu* 煉一還無 ("refining the One to revert to Non-Being")

*liaoming* 了命 ("fulfilling Life")

*liaoxing* 了性 ("fulfilling Nature")

*lingguang* 靈光 (Numinous Radiance)

*lingque* 靈闕 (Numinous Portal)

*Lingshu jing* 靈樞經 (Book of the Numinous Pivot)

*lingyao* 靈藥 (Numinous Medicine)

Liu Haichan 劉海蟾

Liu Qiaoqiao 劉敲蹺 (1839–1933)

*liu wu jiu ji* 流戊就己 ("drifting Wu 戊 to reach Ji 己")

Liu Yiming 劉一明 (1734–1821)

*liuzei* 六賊 ("six thieves")

Longmen 龍門

Lü Dongbin 呂洞賓

*luche* 鹿車 ("deer chariot")

*lulu* 轆轤 (Pulley)

Ma Danyang 馬丹陽 (1123–84)

*Maiwang* 脈望 (The Essence)

*maoyou muyu* 卯酉沐浴 ("bathing at Mao 卯 and You 酉")

*mei* 媒 ("go-between")

*meipo* 媒婆 ("match-maker")

*mianmian ruocun* 綿綿若存 ("unceasing and continuous")

Min Yide 閔一得 (1748–1836)

Ming 命 (Life, Existence)

*mingguan* 命關 (Barrier of Life)

*mingmen* 命門 (Gate of Life)

*mingtang* 明堂 (Hall of Lights)

*mingxin jianxing* 明心見性 ("enlightening one's mind and seeing one's Nature")

*muyu* 沐浴 ("bathing")

*najia* 納甲 (Matching the Stems)

Nanzong 南宗 (Southern Lineage)

*nei huxi* 內呼吸 ("internal breathing")

Neidan 內丹 (Internal Elixir; Internal Alchemy)

*neiguan* 內觀 (inner contemplation)

*Neijia quanfa* 內家拳法 (Martial Arts of the Secret Schools)

*neiqi* 內氣 (internal Breath)

*neishi* 內視 (inner observation)

*neiyao* 內藥 (Internal Medicine)

*ni* 逆 ("inverting the course")

*niuche* 牛車 ("ox chariot")

*niwan gong* 泥丸宮 (Palace of the Muddy Pellet)

*niwan* 泥丸 (Muddy Pellet)

*nixing chengxian* 逆行成仙 ("inverting the course generates an Immortal")

*nixing* 逆行 ("inverting the course")

Peng Si 彭耜 (fl. 1217–51)

Penghu 蓬壺

*qian santian, hou sanguan* 前三田, 後三關 ("three Fields in the front, three Barriers in the back")

*qianding* 乾頂 (Summit of Qian ☰)

*qianding* 乾鼎 (Qian ☰ Tripod)

*qiangong* 乾宮 (Palace of Qian ☰)

*Qianlong Dazang jing* 乾隆大藏經 (Buddhist Canon of the Qianlong Emperor)

*qianqi [zhi] yunxing* 潛氣[之]運行 ("circulation of the hidden Breath")

*Qiaoqiao dongzhang* 敲蹻洞章 (Writings from the Cavern of Liu Qiaoqiao)

Qigong 氣功

*qijing* 奇經 ("extraordinary channels," or vessels)

*qijing bamai* 奇經八脈 (eight "extraordinary vessels")

"Qijing bamai kao" 奇經八脈考 ("An Investigation of the Eight Extraordinary Vessels")

*Qinghua biwen* 青華秘文 (Secret Text of Green Florescence)

*qingjing* 清靜 (clarity and quiescence)

Qingxia zi 青霞子

*qingxiu pai* 清修派 (Pure Cultivation branch)

Qiu Chuji 丘處機 (1148–1227)

*qixue* 氣穴 (Cavity of Breath)

*qizhi zhi xing* 氣質之性 (temperament)

*qu kan tian li* 取坎填離 ("taking from Kan ☵ in order to fill Li ☲")

*Quan Tang shi* 全唐詩 (Complete Poetry of the Tang)

Quanzhen 全真

*queqiao* 鵲橋 (Magpie Bridge)

*qukuang liujin* 去礦留金 ("eliminating the ore to keep the gold")

*rangu xue* 然谷穴 (Blazing Valley cavity)

*renmai* 任脈 (Function vessel)

*renxin* 人心 (human mind)

*rouqi* 柔氣 ("soft breath")

*ruding* 入定 ("entering stability")

*ruhuan* 入環 ("entering the enclosure")

*rujing* 入靜 (entering the state of quiescence)

*Ruyao jing* 入藥鏡 (Mirror for Compounding the Medicine)

*sanbao* 三寶 (Three Treasures)

*sanche yunzhuan* 三車運轉 ("turning around the Three Chariots") *sanhua juding* 三花聚頂 ("the three flowers gather at the sinciput")

*sanjiao heyi* 三教合一 (unity of the Three Teachings)

*sanquan* 三全 ("the three wholes")

*sanyuan* 三元 (Three Origins)

*shangde* 上德 ("superior virtue")

*shangguan* 上關 ("higher barrier")

*Shangqing ji* 上清集 (Collection of Highest Clarity)

Shao Yong 邵雍 (1012–77)

*shaoyin* 少陰 (Minor Yin)

*shen* 神 (Spirit)

*shen* 身 (body, person)

*shen wai shen* 身外身 ("a body outside the body")

*shengke* 生克 ("generation and conquest")

*shengming li* 生命力 (life force)

*shengsi qiao* 生死竅 (Opening of Life and Death)

*shengtai* 聖胎 (Embryo of Sainthood)

Shi Tai 石太 (?–1158)

*shi'er xiaoxi* 十二消息 ("twelve-stage ebb and flow")

*Shihan ji* 石函記 (Records from a Stone Casket)

*shijie* 尸解 ("liberation from the corpse")

*shishen* 識神 ("cognitive spirit")

*shiyue guan* 十月關 (Barrier of the Ten Months)

*shouqiao* 守竅 ("guarding the Opening")

*shouxin* 收心 ("collecting the mind")

*shouyi* 守一 ("guarding Unity")

*shouzhong* 守中 ("guarding the Center")

*shuifu* 水府 (Palace of Water)

*shun* 順 ("following the course")

*shunhua* 順化 ("continuing transformation")

*si koujue* 四口訣 ("the four oral instructions")

*sida* 四大 (four elements)

*sihu* 死戶 (Door of Death)

*Siku tiyao* 四庫提要 (Descriptive Notes on the Books of the Four Repositories)

*sizheng muyu* 四正沐浴 ("bathing at the four cardinal points")

*sizheng* 四正 (four cardinal points)

*Sizhu Wuzhen pian* 四注悟真篇 (Four Commentaries to *Awakening to Reality*)

*suanyao guilu* 送藥歸爐 ("delivering the Medicine to the stove")

*Taiji tu shoushou kao* 太極圖授受考 (Study of the *Transmission of the Chart of the Ultimate*)

*taixi* 胎息 ("embryonic breathing")

*Taixi jing* 胎息經 (Scripture of Embryonic Breathing)

*Taixi jing zhu* 胎息經注 (Commentary to the *Scripture of Embryonic Breathing*)

*Taixi ming* 胎息銘 (Inscription on Embryonic Breathing)

*tiangan* 天干 (celestial stems)

*tiangen* 天根 (Heaven's Root)

*tiangong* 天宮 (Celestial Palace)

*tiangu* 天谷 (Heaven's Valley)

*tianjing* 天經 (Heaven's Warp)

*tianmen* 天門 (Gate of Heaven)

*tianshu* 天樞 (Celestial Axis)

*Tianxian zhengli zhilun* 天仙正理直論 (Straightforward Discourses on the Correct Principles of Celestial Immortality)

*tianzhen* 天真 (Celestial Reality)

*tiao zhenxi* 調真息 ("harmonizing the true breathing")

*tiaojing* 調精 ("harmonizing the Essence")

*tiaoshen* 調神 ("harmonizing the Spirit")

*tiaoxi* 調息 ("harmonizing the breathing")

*Tingxin zhai kewen* 聽心齋客問 (Answers to a Guest at the Studio of Listening to the Heart)

*tong rendu* 通任督 ("clearing the Function and Control vessels")

*tong sanguan* 通三關 ("clearing the three Barriers")

*tongguan* 通關 ("clearing of the barriers")

*tufu* 土釜 ("earthenware crucible")

*tui yinfu* 退陰符 ("withdrawing by the Yin response")

*tuifu* 退符 ("withdrawing in response")

*tuoyue gongfu* 橐籥功夫 ("practice of the bellows")

Waidan 外丹 (External Elixir; External Alchemy)

"Waipian" 外篇 ("Outer Chapters")

*waiyao* 外藥 (External Medicine)

Wan Shangfu 萬尚父 (Ming dynasty)

Wang Bangshu 王邦叔 (fl. ca. 1075)

Wang Haicang 王海藏 (Yuan dynasty)

Wang Jinchan 王金蟾 (thirteenth century)

*wei* 危 (Rooftop, lunar mansion)

Wei Boyang 魏伯陽

*weilü* 尾閭 (Caudal Funnel)

Weng Baoguang 翁葆光 (fl. 1173)

wenhuo 文火 ("gentle fire" or "civil fire")

*wenyang* 溫養 ("nourishing warmly")

*wo* 我 (the "self")

Wu Shouyang 伍守陽 (1574–1644)

*wu* 無 ("nothing")

*wuhuo* 武火 ("fierce fire" or "martial fire")

*wuji* 無極 (Ultimateless)

*Wuji tu* 無極圖 (Chart of the Ultimateless)

*wujue* 無覺 (non-perception)

*wulou* 無漏 ("uncontaminated")

*wuqi chaoyuan* 五氣朝元 ("return of the five agents to the source")

*wushu* 巫術 (shamanic and mediumistic arts)

*wuwei* 無為 ("non-doing")

*wuxing* 五行 (five agents)

*Wuzhen pian* 悟真篇 (Awakening to Reality)

*Wuzhen pian chanyou* 悟真篇闡幽 (Clarification of Obscurities in *Awakening to Reality*)

*Wuzhen pian shiyi* 悟真篇拾遺 (Supplement to *Awakening to Reality*)

*Wuzhen zhizhi* 悟真直指 (Straightforward Directions on *Awakening to Reality*)

*Wuzhen zhizhi xiangshuo sansheng biyao* 悟真直指詳說三乘祕要 (Straightforward Directions and Detailed Explanations on *Awakening to Reality* and the Secret Essentials of the Three Vehicles)

*Wuzhen pian zhushu* 悟真篇註疏 (Commentary and Subcommentary to *Awakening to Reality*)

*xiade* 下德 ("inferior virtue")

*Xian Fo hezong yulu* 仙佛合宗語錄 (Recorded Sayings on the Common Origin of the Immortals and the Buddhas)

*xianshu* 仙術 (arts of Immortality)

*xiantian* 先天(precelestial, "prior to Heaven")

*xiantian jing* 先天精 (precelestial Essence; Essence prior to Heaven)

*xiantian qi* 先天炁 (precelestial Breath; Breath prior to Heaven)

*xiao dinglu* 小鼎爐 ("Small Tripod and Stove")

Xiao Tingzhi 肖廷芝 (fl. 1260–64)

*xiao zhoutian* 小周天 (Lesser Celestial Circuit)

*xiaoxi* 消息 ("ebb and flow")

*xin* 心 (Heart; heart; mind)

*xing* 刑 ("punishment")

*xing* 形 (form)

Xing 性 (Nature)

*Xingming guizhi* 性命圭旨 (Teachings on the Joint Cultivation of Nature and Life)

*xinxing* 心性 (Nature of the Mind)

*Xishan qunxian huizhen ji* 西山群真會真記 (Records of the Immortals and the True Men of the Western Mountain)

*Xiuzhen shishu* 修真十書(Ten Books on the Cultivation of Reality)

*Xiyou ji* 西遊記 (Journey to the West)

Xu Xun 許遜 (trad. 239–374)

*xu* 虛 (Emptiness, lunar mansion)

*xuanguan* 玄關 (Mysterious Barrier)

*xuanguan yiqiao* 玄關一竅 (One Opening of the Mysterious Barrier)

*xuanmiao ji* 玄妙機 ("mysterious and wondrous mechanism")

*xuanpin* 玄牝 (Mysterious-Female)

*xuanpin zhi men* 玄牝之門 (Gate of the Mysterious-Female)

*xuanxuan* 玄玄 ("mystery upon mystery")

Xuanzhong zi 玄中子

*xubi* 虛比 ("empty similitude")

*xuwei xue* 虛危穴 (Emptiness-Rooftop cavity)

*xuwu* 虛無 (Emptiness and Non-Being)

*yang qiaomai* 陽蹻脈 (Yang Heel vessel)

*yang weimai* 陽維脈 (Yang Linking vessel)

*yangche* 羊車 ("sheep chariot")

*yangguang* 陽光 (Yang radiance)

*yangguang sanxian* 陽光三現 ("three appearances of the Yang radiance")

*yangshen* 陽神 (Yang Spirit)

*yangsheng* 養生 (Nourishing Life)

*yao* 藥 (Medicine)

Ye Wenshu 葉文叔 (twelfth century)

*yi* 意 (Intention)

*yiding* 移鼎 ("moving the tripod")

*Yijing* 周易 (Book of Changes)

*yin qiaomai* 陰蹻脈 (Yin Heel vessel)

*yin qiaoxue* 陰蹻穴 (Yin Heel cavity)

*yin weimai* 陰維脈 (Yin Linking vessel)

Yin Zhiping 尹志平 (1169–1251)

*yinfu* 陰符 ("Yin response")

*Yinfu jing* 陰符經 (Scripture of the Hidden Agreement)

*ying'er* 嬰兒 (Infant)

*yinlu* 飲露 ("drinking dew")

*yinshen* 陰神 (Yin Spirit)

*Yinshi zi jingzuo fa* 因是子靜坐法 (Method of Sitting in Quiescence of Master Yinshi)

Yinyang pai 陰陽派 (Yin-Yang branch)

*yiqi* 一炁 (One Breath)

*yishen* 一神 (One Spirit)

*yishen buxin* 以腎補心 ("using the kidneys to replenish the heart")

*yitai* 移胎 ("moving the embryo")

*yitu* 意土 (Intention-Soil)

*Yiwai biezhuan* 易外別傳 (The Separate Transmission of the *Book of Changes*)

*yiyang sheng* 一陽生 ("birth of initial Yang")

*yong* 用 (operation)

142

*yongquan* 湧泉 (Bubbling Spring)

*you you ru wu* 由有入無 ("entering from Being into Non-Being")

*youwei* 有為 ("doing")

*youzuo* 有作 ("doing")

Yu Yan 俞琰 (1258–1314)

*yuan* 元 ("original")

*yuanjing* 元精 (Original Essence)

*yuanliao* 原料 (*prima materia*)

*yuanshen* 元神 (Original Spirit)

*yuanshi zuqi zhi qiao* 元始祖炁之竅 (Opening of the Original Ancestral Breath)

*yuanshi* 元始 (Origin)

*yudu* 玉都 (Jade Capital)

*yueku xue* 月窟穴 (Cavity of the Moon's Lair)

*yuhu* 玉壺 (Jade Pot)

*yuhua* 羽化 ("winged transformation")

Yuhuang 玉皇 (Jade Sovereign)

*yujing shan* 玉京山 (Mountain of the Jade Capital)

*Yuqing jinsi Qinghua biwen jinbao neilian danjue* 玉清金笥青華秘文金寶內煉丹
訣 (Alchemical Instructions on the Inner Refinement of the Golden
Treasure, a Secret Text from the Golden Casket of the Jade Clarity Transmitted by the Immortal of Green Florescence)

*Yuxuan yulu* 御選語錄 (Imperial Compilation of Recorded Sayings)

*yuzhen* 玉枕 (Jade Pillow)

*zanian* 雜念 (impure thoughts)

*zengjian* 增減 ("augmenting and decreasing")

Zhang Boduan 張伯端 (987?–1082)

Zhao Taiding 趙台鼎 (Ming dynasty)

*zhen zhongzi* 真種子 (True Seed)

*zhengjing* 正經 ("ordinary channels")

*zhenjing* 真精 (True Essence)

*zhenqi* 真氣 (True Breath)

*Zhenquan* 真詮 (The Ultimate Truth)

*zhenyi* 真意 (True Intention)

*zhiguan* 止觀 ("cessation and contemplation")

*zhinian* 止念 (ceasing thoughts)

*Zhixuan pian* 指玄篇 (Pointing to the Mystery)

Zhong-Lü 鐘呂

*Zhong-Lü chuandao ji* 鐘呂傳道集 (Records of the Transmission of the Dao
from Zhongli Quan to Lü Dongbin)

*zhongguan* 中關 ("intermediate barrier")

*Zhonghe ji* 中和集 (Collection of Central Harmony)

*zhonghuang* 中黃 (Central Yellow)

Zhongli Quan 鐘離權

*zhongshi* 種室 ("chamber of the seed")

*zhongtian huaitai* 中田懷胎 ("pregnancy in the middle Cinnabar Field")

*zhongxi* 踵息 ("breathing through the heels")

Zhu Yizun 朱彝尊 (1629–1709)

Zhu Yuanyu 朱元育 (fl. 1657–69)

*zhu* 主 (ruler)

*Zhuangzi* 莊子 (Book of Master Zhuang Zhou)

*zhuji* 築基 ("laying the foundations")

*zifu* 紫府 (Purple Prefecture)

*ziran* 自然 ("spontaneous, natural, so of its own")

*ziru* 自如 ("spontaneous, natural, so of its own")

*zuichu huanxu* 最初還虛 ("earliest return to Emptiness")

*zuichu lianji gongfu* 最初煉己功夫 ("earliest practice of self-refining")

*zuo dayao* 做大藥 (Compounding the Great Medicine)

*zuodan* 做丹 (Compounding the Elixir)

*zuoguan* 坐關 ("barrier of sitting")

*zuqi xue* 祖氣穴 (Cavity of the Ancestral Breath)

*zuqiao* 祖竅 ("ancestral opening")

# AWAKENING TO REALITY

*The "Regulated Verses" of the Wuzhen pian,
a Taoist Classic of Internal Alchemy*

FABRIZIO PREGADIO

*Awakening to Reality*
*The "Regulated Verses" of the* Wuzhen pian,
*a Taoist Classic of Internal Alchemy*

Translated by Fabrizio Pregadio

Golden Elixir Press, 2009, viii + 102 pp.
ISBN 978-0984308217, Paperback and PDF

www.goldenelixir.com

*Awakening to Reality* (*Wuzhen pian*) is one of the most important and best-known Taoist alchemical texts. Written in the eleventh century, it describes in a poetical form several facets of Neidan, or Internal Alchemy. This book presents the first part of the text, consisting of sixteen poems, which contain a concise but comprehensive exposition of Neidan. In addition to notes that intend to clarify the meaning of the more obscure points, the book also contains selections from a commentary dating from the late eighteenth century, which is distinguished by the use of a lucid and plain language.

Golden Elixir Press

www.goldenelixir.com
info@goldenelixir.com

Golden Elixir Press publishes dependable and affordable books
on Taoism, Taoist alchemy, and other traditional doctrines,
both in print and as e-books.

Isabelle Robinet, *Essays on Taoist Internal Alchemy*. Forthcoming.

Wang Mu, *Foundations of the Internal Elixir: The Taoist Practice of Neidan*. 2011.

Ananda K. Coomaraswamy, *Hinduism and Buddhism*. 2011.

Jami, *Flashes of Light: A Treatise on Sufism*. 2010.

Shaikh Sharfuddin Maneri, *Letters from a Sufi Teacher*. 2010.

Fabrizio Pregadio, *Awakening to Reality: The "Regulated Verses" of the Wuzhen pian, a Taoist Classic of Internal Alchemy*. 2009.

Fabrizio Pregadio, *Chinese Alchemy: An Annotated Bibliography of Works in Western Languages*. 2009.

Fabrizio Pregadio, *Index of Zhonghua Daozang*. 2009.

CPSIA information can be obtained at www.ICGtesting.com
Printed in the USA
BVOW05s0832171215

430531BV00003B/258/P